Manifest and Invest

Manifest
AND
Invest

—

Live Your
BEST LIFE
Get Your
MONEY RIGHT

Dawn Santoriello, CFP®

Manifest AND Invest

Live Your Best Life Get Your Money Right

Printed in the United States of America

Advisory Services offered by Attleboro Wealth Management.

Chapter on Manifestation offered by Dawn Santoriello Enterprises.

First Edition

ISBN 979-8-218-19419-2 paperback
ISBN 979-8-218-19420-8 ebook
Library of Congress Control Number: 2023907439

Cover and Interior Design by:
Chris Treccani

Created with the Book to Millions® Method

CONTENTS

Part 1: Setting the Stage for Abundance   1

Chapter 1: Clearing the Path to Abundance   3

Chapter 2: How to Have a Good Relationship with
Money—Daily Habits   13

Chapter 3: My Story   19

Chapter 4: A Powerful Manifestation Technique to
Clear Your Money Blocks   27

Chapter 5: Releasing the Five Biggest Money Blocks   35

Chapter 6: What Money Block Do You Have?   43

Chapter 7: The Five Different Money Personality Types   53

Part 2: How to Save   57

Chapter 8: What Makes Me Qualified to Give
Financial Advice?   59

Chapter 9: Women and Money   63

Chapter 10: Saving Money Made Easy   71

Chapter 11: Getting and Staying Out of Debt   75

Part 3: What to Do Once You Have Money   83

Chapter 12: How to Invest in the Stock Market   85

Chapter 13: One Of the Best Places to Save Your Money   107

Chapter 14: How to Use Your Overfunded Life
Insurance Policy as Your Bank   117
Chapter 15: Protection Against Market Volatility   135

End Notes   141
Acknowledgements   147
About the Author   149
Help me inspire and educate others!   151

This book is dedicated to you.
You have unlimited possibilities... live your best life!

Part 1
Setting the Stage for Abundance

CHAPTER 1

Clearing the Path to Abundance

—————

Everything in your life is interconnected. The current state of your finances is a window into what is going on in your world—into your personal relationships and your job. How you do *one* thing is how you do *everything*. The good news is, once you clean up your finances, other areas of your life should get better as well.

I learned a very important lesson in life at age 19. I was in a job I loathed, and I noticed that I was miserable in *all* areas of my life. Once I started doing work that I enjoyed, the rest of my life improved.

Sometimes we aren't fortunate enough to be doing what we love. If you fall into this category, just keep moving forward in the direction you want to go, no matter how small your steps are. Keep taking action. Focus on what is working well in your current situation. Don't blame yourself for your money issues, because that will just create more negativity and keep you stuck in a mentality of scarcity.

It's good to accept where you are right now. Maybe you're not exactly working at your dream job. That's okay—it's a step toward where you want to be. Sometimes you have to go sideways to go forward. You may have to do some things you don't want to do in order to get to your dream job. Keep taking action, keep praying, and realize that you are abundant, and watch what happens. Commit to abundance today and watch your life change. This is the time to go see a financial planner to help you get back on track.

You have tremendous power within you. Your mindset has a huge impact on your life. Your thoughts—what you tell yourself about money—can keep you in a state of lack or abundance. We cover clearing money blocks in Chapter 6.

I'm sure you've heard the saying, "Money attracts money." I encourage you to start saving and investing—start today. You can set aside $10, $100, or $1,000 a week—whatever you have available right now. This practice will energetically attract more money to you. You have the thought, "I want more money." You take action by saving and investing money, and you receive more money through compound interest. You are in receiving mode, and you may even receive money from unexpected places.

Everybody has a story about money. What is your money story? Today is the day to start rewriting your money story if it isn't working for you. To start rewriting, make a list of smart money decisions you have made. For example, perhaps you bought an investment property that is profitable or that you made profitable. Next, write down what you learned from that situation. Then, write down your financial losses or mistakes. Maybe you invested in a business, and it failed. That's okay. What did you learn from that experience, and what can you do to improve the next time you invest? Last, write down everything you believe about money.

Your current money story may be so engrained in your sub-conscious that you have to do some clearing out before you actually believe the new story you just created. Many of our money stories date back to childhood, and they may not even be our own. As children, we accepted what our parents or other adults said as our own truth:

- "Money doesn't grow on trees."
- "Money is the root of all evil."
- "The harder I work, the more money I will make."

Money itself is energy. The energy is neutral until we apply our story to it. The story we apply to the energy, whether positive or negative, will manifest itself in our life.

A perfect example of this can be seen with lottery winners. Most lottery winners lose everything they win within two years. How is possible to lose millions of dollars? Easy. Some people don't think they are worthy of having a lot of money and/or are bad at managing their money. You may have the belief that money goes out just as fast as it comes in. Have you had that thought before?

Unless you stop the cycle of unhealthy thoughts about money, your situation will not improve. After reading this book, you will know how to make smart money moves. In Chapter 4, I will teach you a powerful manifestation technique that will clear, heal, and change your negative money beliefs.

Here is an example of a money belief and how to change it:

"If I have a lot of money, I won't have good friends, because people will just use me for my money. They will always make me pick up the tab, because they know I can easily afford it."

If your friends always make you pick up the tab, they aren't good friends. Change your story to something more positive:

"If I have more money, I can contribute to worthy causes and give back to society. I will attract like-minded friends by my generosity."

Just a small change in your mindset creates a whole new space that allows more abundance into your life. You have the power to change your life. And by the way—you're the *only* one that can change your life.

You might be thinking, "My situation is hopeless." Never give up hope. You *can* change your life. Joe Vitale, who was featured in the movie *The Secret*, was homeless and living on the streets at one point, but he became a multimillionaire. He had no money to begin with, but he took action. He went to the library and read books like Napoleon Hill's *Think and Grow Rich*. He worked on himself and changed his beliefs about money. Today, he helps other people through his coaching and has authored several books. If he can do it, so can you.

I love one of Anthony Hopkins' lines from the movie, *The Edge*: "What one man can do, another can do." Nothing is impossible. No matter where you're standing right now, you can accomplish anything. So please, never lose hope. Hope sparks everything.

You also need to have faith. It doesn't matter what you call it, but you need to have faith in a Higher Power—God, the Universe, the Divine.

Now, let's clear the money blocks that are holding you back from allowing more abundance into your life.

Thank You, God, for this for me. Clearing the blockages that are holding me back financially so I can allow more abundance into my life, live a better lifestyle, and do the things I want to do. Release all the conscious and subconscious beliefs I have about money that keep me stuck in lack. Release any other unhealthy thoughts about money and provide me with a healthy flow of money gently and easily in the best way for me and all or something better. And thank you God for that for me. Love Energy, clear, heal, and change anything keeps this prayer from being answered, and let me be happy no matter what happens. And thank you God for that for me.

Now you say, "And thank you God for that for me."

Some of you might be saying, "This isn't going to work for me. I am in a dead-end job." If that's your case, I have an exercise for you. Create your dream job—write down every detail of what the job is. Include everything—salary, benefits, location, what your workday looks like, how many vacation days you get. Keep going until you can envision it clearly. Read your description when you wake up in the morning and before you go to bed at night. If you hear a negative voice in your head, take your dream job description out and read it. The current negativity in your mind is not serving you, so take this opportunity to change. When one door closes, another door opens. Since we can't see the door, we are creating the door through this exercise. Say the prayer over the job you created and watch the miracle that happens.

You have to follow up on the signs the Universe sends you and take action. You can't just sit on your ass and expect a job to fall in your lap without action. There are no coincidences in this world. Just happening to run into an ex-coworker at the coffee shop you went to today because your usual coffee shop was closed was *not* an accident. She may know of a position at her company that is your dream job. Or she may know someone who is hiring, and you may be a perfect fit. The action you need to take is to open your mouth and have a conversation with her. Don't just nod and not say anything to her.

I was once in a similar situation. I was in a career I loved, but I wasn't enjoying the success I knew I was capable of. I had to humble myself to take on side jobs, including bartending and doing manual labor for a neighbor. Though it was painful and embarrassing at times, I never lost sight of the abundance that was coming my way. And the abundance *did* come. I went from having $200 in my bank account to earning a six-figure income that year. I hope you glean inspiration from this.

No one can be positive all the time. We are only human, and negative thoughts creep in every now and then. The key is to not get stuck in these thoughts, because we are powerful manifestors and we will attract more negativity if we think unhealthy thoughts.

In early June 2022, I brought my car in to the dealer because my key fob wasn't working properly. While I was waiting, I looked around the showroom. There was a beautiful 2022 Lexus RC 300 F Sport. It was white, with a white and black leather interior.

(My car was a 2017 model that I named "Lexi." I loved her to the day she was declared deceased. I'll get to that shortly.)

I thought, "This white Lexus is gorgeous. I want it." I didn't really want it, because I didn't want to have a car payment again—I had just finished paying off Lexi. But if someone *gave* me the new Lexus, I would gladly accept it.

Over the Fourth of July weekend and the week that followed, I was in a real funk.

It had all started when I moved back to Yardley, Pennsylvania, in August 2021. I had lived there from 2015 to 2018, and I was always trying to get away from the area during that time. Yardley is pretty, but it's geared toward married couples with kids, not a single adventurous woman. I should have stayed where I was in King of Prussia, Pennsylvania, but my landlord had raised my rent by $300, wasn't open to negotiating, and wanted an answer in five days.

I turned to a spiritual advisor. She said I should move, that it would be good for me. Although my intuition told me to stay put, I took her advice and moved to Yardley— actually, I moved back into the same apartment I had in 2018. *That* was a sign.

By July 2022, after almost a year back in Yardley, I was really down as the Fourth of July weekend approached, because none of my friends lived in Yardley and everyone had plans. Friends were off celebrating in the Hamptons, having barbecues, going to parties, and going to the beach. I felt so lonely.

I thought, "This is not the life I am supposed to be living. I want to be out having fun and enjoying the weekend. I want to be out on a boat somewhere. I want to live in a place that has a lot to offer in terms of the outdoors but is still near a clean city and close to an airport. I want to have interesting conversations with people." None of these things were happening for me at the moment.

I got stuck on all the things that *weren't* happening for me, everything I was missing out on. I went into a really dark place that week; I'm going to be vulnerable and share it with you. I felt like no one needed me. It's very lonely to feel like you aren't needed, especially when you are a social person like me. I wondered, "Is this how my life is going to be? Will I be bored for the rest of my life?"

My thoughts weren't true at all, but when you are facing your shadows you can't see the light. I had plenty to be grateful for. I have a great boyfriend; we share a wonderful connection, and he is so supportive. I have wonderful friends and family. I went on two trips to the Bahamas earlier this year, and I am going to Italy in the fall. After struggling in my career, I am now experiencing success. My last book was a bestseller on Amazon. What right did I have to cry that my life sucked just because I was occasionally bored and lonely and couldn't decide where to live?

When we're down, we often think, "This is the way it's always going to be." But it's not. The next Saturday my cousin and I were commiserating about our boredom and agreeing that we needed more fun in our lives. We are both in our 40s and unmarried; many people our age are married with kids and don't have free time like we do. My cousin lives in Long Island; otherwise, we would be doing things together every weekend. After commiserating, we did my manifestation technique to clear out any negativity and blockages holding us back from living a fulfilled life.

Well, things happened quickly after that. The next morning, the Universe knocked some sense into me—quite literally. I was in a bad car accident. I was T-boned at an intersection, and my car was pushed into oncoming traffic. Out of the corner of my eye, I saw a white Jeep Grand Cherokee coming toward me, and I thought to myself, "This car isn't stopping. They are blowing the red light." Then came the boom of the impact and the sound of glass shattering on me. It was the scariest moment of my life. I quickly jumped out of the car screaming, crying, and shaking. I could have died or broken bones, could have been in a coma or paralyzed. (I was also crying because I just paid off Lexi. I loved her and wasn't ready to let her go.) It was an absolute miracle that I only had surface scrapes from the glass and a sore back, shoulders, and neck. I am so grateful to be alive and I am no longer bored. Each day on earth is a gift. We take many things for granted—until we get a wake-up call. When I got out of the hospital, I felt a stillness and inner peace that I'd never felt before.

I learned from my accident that yes, I am needed, and many people care about me. It's not necessary for every day to be filled with activities. On the days when I have nothing to do and am bored, I can count my blessings and be grateful for everything I have. We can use such times for self-reflection. Not every day is meant to be exciting; if life were that way, we would burn out. We need quiet alone time to balance our lives. Don't worry—there are many days ahead filled with adventure and excitement.

Unfortunately, I received the sad news that Lexi was totaled. I ended up getting a new car, although it was a different model from the one I had seen at the dealership in June, the 2022 Lexus RC 300 F Sport. I test-drove the RC 300 F Sport and the IS 350 F Sport, and the latter felt better on my back, so I went with that model.

It's nearly impossible to get cars these days. I told the salesperson at the dealership I wanted it in white with a white/black leather interior. He checked and said one had just come off the truck and was being inspected. We went to look at it and I said, "That's my car." He told me that if I made a deposit, it was mine.

So, I did get a brand-new car, just not in the way I expected. I definitely don't recommend the path I took to anyone. My negativity had helped create the conditions for my accident. I have all the tools and resources at my disposal to avoid that kind of negativity. But even people like me, who preach positivity, sometimes stumble.

We are all human; we are not perfect. Logic sometimes flies out the window, and our emotions take over. We like to believe we are in control of our emotions, but that is not true. As soon as you hear negative chatter in your head and start thinking bad thoughts, ask yourself, "Is this true? Is this one hundred percent true? How do I feel when I have this thought? Where would I be if I never had this thought?" Then, turn the thought around and make it positive. By changing your beliefs, you change your life. I learned this technique from my friends Jesse and Genia, who changed many lives through their work as trauma coaches.

After having some sense *literally* knocked into me, I found opportunities all around me. I got a brand-new car. I got an invite to a party. Someone offered me a business opportunity that involved speaking to groups, which I love to do.

Remember, it's okay to get stuff wrong. You are on your own journey. If you fall, just pick yourself up and try again.

CHAPTER 2

How to Have a Good Relationship with Money—Daily Habits

—

Your relationship with money is like any other relationship—it needs to be nurtured and cared for in order to grow. There must be integrity and honesty in how you treat your money—in your behavior toward money, in your thoughts about money, and in your money habits. You need to respect money. Although this is a book on finance, this chapter may improve not only your relationship with money but *all* the relationships in your life.

The biggest hurdle you need to overcome related to money is *fear*. We feel fear when false evidence appears real. This book will provide you with the tools to manage your money better and clear your money blocks. I want you to gain confidence in how to invest your money—that's why I focus so much on mindset. And of course, as a CERTIFIED FINANCIAL PLANNER™, I am qualified to give financial advice.

Fear holds us back in so many areas of our lives. If we fear being cheated on or abandoned in our romantic relationships, that is exactly what we experience. What we are thinking about, consciously or subconsciously, manifests in our lives. We can control conscious thoughts by replacing negative thoughts with positive thoughts and emotions. To deal with subconscious thoughts, we have to deal with and clear out past traumas and the stories we have created around those traumas.

How do you know if you have subconscious blocks? That's easy. Do you always find yourself in the same situation? Then you have a block related to that scenario.

Are you afraid of actually having money? Do you fear looking at your investment statement because the market is down? Do you believe things about money based on what your parents believed or based on reading information from an unreliable source? Half the stuff that keeps us scared just isn't true. Once you know the truth, fear disappears.

My aim is that this book will take away your money fears.

If you work with a competent professional who communicates with you regularly, and if you are clear about the plan for your money and why it is invested the way it is, you won't be afraid to open your investment statement. You'll know that your plan is built to handle any market condition.

As a CFP®, I am happy to say that during this down year of 2022, my clients haven't called me. They understand that market fluctuations are normal, and they have confidence in me and in the plans we've created together. I educate them ahead of time on what can happen with their money. I've gained many new clients this year because their previous advisors were missing in action. I've also had quite a few prospective clients come to me with portfolios that weren't aligned with their risk tolerance. Some portfolios were concentrated in a few stocks. Some prospects were paying high fees. Most of them were unaware of any of these things until I pointed them out. If you would like me to review your portfolio, reach out to me on my website, dsfinancialstrategies.com.

When you reduce the fear you feel related to money, you can relax and spend time enjoying life instead of worrying. Worrying leads to financial stress, which leads to poor health. I don't want that for you. I want you to live a life you love and to experience financial freedom. To achieve these goals, you need a healthy mindset, body, and soul.

Many people ask me how I deal with stress and are interested in my daily routine. What works for me may or may not work for you. I used to be constantly stressed and worried. I didn't have healthy eating habits. Every day at 3 p.m., I had a donut from Dunkin Donuts.

One day I met with a prospective client, a health coach. He turned the tables on me—I became his client. At first, I thought, "I don't have a problem. I'm not overweight." The truth is, I was a skinny fat person and didn't know it, because I looked healthy on the outside. I wasn't sleeping well, and I was always stressing. Your finances may follow the same pattern—they may look good on the outside but be unhealthy underneath.

With my coach's help, I kicked my donut habit and became healthier. I turned around so much that I now help my financial planning clients with their health and well-being.

I start my day by making my bed as soon as I get up. This sets the tone for my day. Then, I drink a green smoothie. While getting ready for work, I listen to podcasts. (I am a big fan of Andrew Huberman and Peter Crone these days.) For breakfast, I have a protein shake; I have another one for lunch. If it fits in my schedule, I do a 10- to 20-minute yoga nidra session.

Yoga nidra has many health benefits—it reduces stress, induces better sleep, and decreases chronic pain. Yoga nidra is a form of meditation, so anyone can do it. I find different yoga nidra meditations on YouTube. If I don't have time during the day, I spend some time meditating before I go to sleep. Yoga nidra is amazing for sleep—when I sleep, I am out cold and stay asleep.

After work, I do Peloton workouts. I work out every day in some form. Throughout my day, I use a manifestation technique (which I will cover in Chapter 4) when I want something to happen. For dinner, I make a healthy meal from Hello Fresh. I'll also use YouTube meditations for abundance, health, and love as needed. That's what my typical day looks like.

I also use affirmations; I post them above my desk. Here are some of my favorites:

- "I am a powerful Goddess who is desired and wanted. Whatever I desire comes to me." (This was given to me by one of my good spiritual friends.)
- "I have wonderful work in a wonderful way, I give wonderful service for wonderful pay." (This is from *The Game of Life and How to Play It*, by Florence Scovel Shinn.[1])
- "Less is more."
- "I'm going to be okay no matter what."

Feel free to use these or make your own. Stick them on your wall, above your desk, or on your bathroom mirror.

Another important technique I use is visualization. If you can see something in your mind, you can achieve it. You will never achieve something you can't see yourself doing or obtain something you can't see yourself having.

Years ago, before I had my own company, I used to visualize running my own company. Every night, I would say, "I am a successful financial planner with my own practice." A few months later, I went out on my own and formed my company, DS Financial Strategies.

Sit down and visualize how you want your finances to be and the work you want to be doing. Consider making a vision board.

One of my greatest manifestations was manifesting an investment property. I had been wanting an investment property, but I didn't have the money for it. One Friday night, I was scrolling through the multiple listing service (MLS) listings, and I saw my house. It was ugly, but I saw potential. I am usually not good at seeing past the ugly, but I knew this house was meant for me. I called my realtor and told her I wanted to see it the next day. She said she didn't work on the weekends. (She probably didn't want to waste her time.) I contacted another realtor who showed me the house. I put in an offer, and it was accepted. I was amazed that a wealthy investor hadn't scooped up this property.

Perhaps one reason why it wasn't snatched by an investor was that it needed extensive work. I more or less rebuilt the entire house from the ground up. Another factor was that it was listed as being in a town with high taxes. I knew the listed town was incorrect. In addition, it was an estate sale, so the buyers were eager to sell. Everything was in my favor. I went from wishing to own a property and to buying one—in a day. That was one of the best investments I have ever made. The mortgage and taxes are $519 a month, and I bring in $2,200 in monthly income. When you are free of your money blocks you can manifest nearly anything you want.

Make a point of surrounding yourself with people who support you and truly want you to succeed. I've had many great mentors and friends. They have helped me when I have been down and celebrated with me when I have been up. In addition, seek out spiritual guidance when you need it.

A big lesson I've learned is to let go and surrender. I can't control everything in my life, and neither can you. When you accept this fact, you will find freedom. Your life will begin to flow, and opportunities will present themselves. I hope you can implement some of these things in things in your life.

CHAPTER 3

My Story

I was born in the Park Slope neighborhood of Brooklyn, New York, in 1978. My family was poor, and my parents were addicted to drugs and alcohol. When I was two years old, my dad died of a drug overdose—at least, that's the story I was told. (Just this year, I learned through a 23andMe DNA test that he wasn't my dad. But that's another story for another time.) My mom was a drug addict and heavy drinker. She wasn't around much, so my grandmother raised my sister and me.

We were so poor that we couldn't afford a dentist when I had a black hole in my front tooth. Thank God it was a baby tooth. Even so, I have fond memories of my time with my grandmother. My favorite meal that my grandmother made for us—a meal I still eat to this day—was egg noodles and cottage cheese with salt and pepper. Most people's reaction to this description is, "Ugh, gross." Try it. It's delicious! My grandmother tried her best to give us healthy meals with what little money she had.

When my grandmother could no longer take care of us, my sister and I were in and out of foster homes. At one point, we lived with my sister's biological father. He didn't like me because I wasn't his, so he would beat me with his belt. Once, he even threw me in a clothes dryer, but I don't remember if he turned it on. The foster homes we lived in weren't much better. One family made my sister and I eat in the kitchen while they sat together in the dining room. We weren't allowed to have anything to drink until we ate all our food.

Fortunately, my sister and I eventually ended up in a great foster home, with a family who ended up adopting us. I was 10 when we were adopted, and I remember that day well. The judge gave my sister and me huge, swirly lollipops, and we went to our favorite diner for breakfast afterward.

I wanted to never be poor again, and I wanted to help other people gain financial security. Early on, I realized the importance of financial stability, especially after my adoptive family provided that kind of stability for me. I wanted to become a financial planner to help people avoid the scary childhood I had.

Even when I was a child, entrepreneurship was in my blood. I took every opportunity I could to earn money. There was an apple tree and a chestnut tree in the backyard, and my dad would pay me and my four sisters 10 cents a bag to pick them. I made sure I hustled and filled the most bags. Sometimes, my dad would take me to his office on Saturdays, and he paid me two dollars an hour to do filing while he worked. When it snowed, I shoveled driveways. I saved my daily lunch money by making my own lunch at home. When I was in high school, I sold Blow Pops that I bought at BJ's Wholesale Club. I would make about 50 dollars a week doing that. When some other kids started selling candy, the school found out and made them stop. I hadn't known we weren't allowed to sell candy if it didn't benefit the school, but I quit before I got caught. As I ran my micro-businesses, I kept a little accounting journal with subaccounts for a car, a house, and CDs (the music kind). I loved watching the accounts grow!

Before I got into financial planning, my first love was acting and modeling. Once I realized that career path was keeping me broke, I made the switch to financial services. I never thought I could love anything besides acting and modeling, but I was wrong. I only wish I had found this career before the age of 26.

You have to love this career, because up to 90 percent of advisors fail within their first year. The rest are just scraping by unless they are lucky enough to land a wealthy client or work alongside a senior partner. I wasn't so lucky. I had to start from scratch.

Most people think that if you are in the financial services industry, you make a lot of money. According to Glassdoor, the average salary is around $120,000.[1] Some people earn way more. If you maintain a lean operation, you can run your business for about $25,000 to $50,000 a year. That doesn't leave much left for everything else when you are starting out. People don't realize that everything you do in this business costs money—marketing, compliance fees, errors and omissions (E&O) insurance, education, technology, office equipment, and so forth. Even if you work as an independent contractor for another company, you pay for these things. When I started out, I paid over $800 per month for a cubicle!

One day early in my career, I didn't have enough money to get out of a parking garage. It was a cold January day, and there was a line of cars forming behind me. My credit card kept getting declined, and I didn't have any cash. In fact, I only had $200 to my name! I hit the call button to summon an attendant, and after five *long* minutes (and an ever-growing line), someone came out and opened the gate for me. It was so embarrassing! Little did I know I would soon have my first six-figure year.

When I got home that night, I cried. With no new clients on the horizon, I didn't know what I was going to do. I was a single woman working in a field where two incomes are better than one. I was in the middle of a housing remodel that was draining my finances. To top it all off, I couldn't even pay to leave a parking garage!

The solution was to get a part-time job where no one would recognize me until business picked up. God forbid that a client would see me, exposing my lack of success (so far, at least). So, I did manual labor for my neighbor, who was also remodeling his house. For $10 an hour, I scraped paint off walls and cabinets, dug in the dirt, and lifted heavy objects.

I couldn't put in many hours, though, because I had to work my day job. So, I tried bartending on the weekends. Working at a successful, popular bar was out of the question, because I might have seen someone I knew. Instead, I took a job at a seedy, corner bar where the owner had allegedly raped someone in the back room. I made sure a friend of mine was always with me at closing time so I wouldn't be alone with the owner. Compared to what bartenders at successful bars brought in, I hardly made anything. After dealing with drunk, perverted men for about two and a half months, my soul couldn't take it anymore, and I quit.

Meanwhile, I was getting a small sale here and there in my financial planning business, but nothing substantial. To help pay for my housing remodel, I took out a personal loan and borrowed some money from my dad. That hurt my pride. I wanted to be able to say that I was the only one in the family who didn't ask my dad for money.

At the time, I thought, "This shouldn't be my life. I'm a financial planner. I know how to create wealth and grow money." I had helped my clients create more money than they thought was possible, but for some reason, I couldn't do it for myself. I was spiritually blocked when it came to money, and none of my analytical skills could save me.

So, like most people, I've been through it.

Removing my money blocks started with a prayer and a vision board. The prayer helped clear my money blocks, opened the doors to wealth, and changed my finances in a way I didn't think was possible.

I didn't know it at the time, but my life was about to change in a big way. A marketing salesman named Rick had been bugging me for four months. I thought he was trying to sell me newsletters, so I ignored him. One day—I'm not sure why—I decided to take his call. He explained that he wasn't trying to sell me newsletters—he helped advisors with marketing, case design, and lead generation. I immediately wished I had answered his call sooner! Being stubborn isn't always a good thing. Because of the cost of his program, I didn't sign up for it. But Rick and I spoke every now and then for the next couple of months.

One day, Rick told me about a conference where I could learn more about an insurance company and get sales ideas for their products. Immediately, I turned it down, because I assumed it would cost too much. When he said his marketing company would cover the full cost—including airfare—I was in. The conference was scheduled for a month or two later.

As luck would have it, shortly after that phone call, I sideswiped a car while driving down my block—I don't have good spatial awareness. My seven-year-old car had 140,000 miles on it, and I had dropped my collision coverage. The following week, with the driver's side scraped up and a dent in my mirror, I went to meet a client at his country club. I tried to hide the damage by parking in what I thought was a secluded spot. It didn't work. My client came in and said, "Dawn, what happened to your car?" Another embarrassing moment.

I went home and prayed that my car would be totaled. What happened next was an absolute miracle. The next morning, in the middle of my yoga class, a guy walked into the studio and asked if anyone had a white car parked out front.

"That's mine," I said. He suggested I take a look at it. When I walked out, I saw that my car had been pushed up on the sidewalk against a pole. The back tire was twisted, and the driver's side now had more than a dent in the mirror; the entire door was dented!

Luckily, I was calm from yoga class, so I didn't immediately freak out. At first, I thought, "How in the world did this just happen?" But then I realized, "OMG, my prayer was just answered!" I was in shock. I don't remember the exact details, but apparently the owner's son and his girlfriend had a fight. She took off in the car and hit my car and two others. My car took the worst of it.

After my yoga class, I went to look at some Hondas and reality set in—I couldn't afford a new car. What was I going to do? Luckily, I didn't have to decide right away, because the next day, I flew to the conference Rick had scheduled me for.

The conference was amazing! I learned a strategy that helped many of my clients. This one new strategy earned me $80,000 in one month! Needless to say, I had my best year ever, earning over six figures!

However, I still had to deal with my car when I returned from the conference. The owner of the other vehicle was a well-known, successful businessman in Scranton, Pennsylvania, and he claimed that his son didn't have permission to use the car. Scranton men think they are above the law, and they are always trying to pull one over on others, especially women. I told the insurance adjuster that what the owner was doing was unjust and that he shouldn't be allowed to escape his obligation to the insurance company. A week later, my car was determined to be totaled, and I received a check for over $7,000—more than what I was expecting!

It gets better. A friend from yoga class suggested we check out Acura's, even though they were out of my price range. I found a fully loaded leftover model for less than I would have paid for the Honda!

Among the many lessons I learned that year, the biggest was to have faith that everything will work out in your favor, no matter how things look initially.

I got into financial planning when my modeling and acting career didn't work out because I had a bachelor's degree in finance and I love helping people. Today, I can't imagine doing anything else. I am so passionate about what I do every day, and I am always learning something new to help my clients. I create programs that help my clients reach their personal and professional goals and motivate them to achieve their dreams. I choose the clients I want to work with and, best of all, I can work anywhere in the world with my laptop and an internet connection.

If you are passionate about something, go for it wholeheartedly and you will reach your goal. Even if you don't reach the exact goal you envisioned, you will be in a better place than you are in today. Don't let the naysayers deter you.

When I decided to enter the insurance field, a friend tried to talk me out of it. She told me her husband was very smart, and he couldn't make it in insurance sales. In fact, most people don't make it in that field. Even my dad told me to find a job that paid a salary instead of the commission-only job I had been offered. He was trying to protect his daughter, as dads do. Being the stubborn daughter I am, I ignored his advice and accepted the job. (My dad eventually came around. When I began working at a well-known company, he told me, "Dawn, don't try to take over the company in six months.") I had never even thought of owning my own business, but 16 years later, here I am, founder of DS Financial Strategies.

My biggest takeaways from my first six-figure year are these:

- Do whatever it takes to make your dreams come true, even if you have to take on a side hustle.
- Don't be closed-minded.
- And of course, don't drop your collision insurance!

CHAPTER 4

A Powerful Manifestation Technique to Clear Your Money Blocks

I met my friend and spiritual teacher Lynn Rene MacDonald a few years ago. I had already embarked on my spiritual journey when I ran into her at a mall. At the time, I was going through a rough period, and I had prayed the night before that God would send me someone who could help me. I woke up that morning and felt the need to go to the mall. I didn't want to go, but when my intuition tells me to do something, I listen.

There was a health fair at the mall that day. I met some really interesting people, and Lynn was one of them. When I approached her, I could tell she was a high-vibing intuitive, and she had great energy. I realized she was the answer to my prayer. Since our meeting at the mall, she has taught me a prayer that has changed my life and has caused miracles to happen for me. She taught me how to create my life and continually clear all my blocks—emotional, financial, spiritual, you name it!

An important thing about the prayer is that once you say it, you have to let it go. Don't dwell on it and try to figure out how things are going to happen—just let it go. Letting go is an extremely important part of the process. If you don't let go, you remain stuck in wanting something and simply manifest more wanting.

The prayer is important when it comes to finances: You want more money, and you have cleared the external blocks that you are aware of. However, your finances are still not quite right, so you call upon Spirit/God/Universe/Love/Energy to clear any subconscious blocks. This kind of prayer solves the problem of being guided by lack and blocking abundance! Some blocks may not clear up instantly, so it's important to continue clearing and praying.

If we rely only on ourselves, we feel stuck and lost when things become difficult. We feel frustrated and panicky. We make mistakes with our money, because we want a certain outcome and we think we know the best way to get it. Money will take over our lives if we block its natural flow by worrying about it too much. It will become all we think about.

How can we break out of such difficulties? With a little help from Spirit and the law of attraction. The law of attraction states that positive thoughts create positive circumstances, and negative thoughts create negative circumstances. When you say the prayer I'm about to share with you in times of unease, stress, or anxiety about money, you will free yourself from worry because you are letting your Higher Power handle it for you. You will be calmer and more receptive to new ideas and inspirations for your finances that Spirit is trying to send you. You will have financial peace of mind and manifest abundance!

Here is the manifestation technique I use. I say:

Thank you, God, for this for me: [insert what you want in the present tense, the more detail the better] in the best way for me and all or something better! And thank you God for that for me. Love Energy, clear, heal, and change anything that would prevent this prayer from being answered, and let me be happy no matter what happens. And thank you God for that for me.

Everything happens in Divine time, not your time. In order to manifest your dreams, you also must be in your heart space. As you progress in your journey, things change as you change. But everything you need to grow is given to you at the right time. Sometimes, you have to experience certain circumstances in order to understand what you do or don't want in your life.

I can't wait to hear about your successes with this powerful technique.

After attending one of my webinars, "Releasing the 5 Biggest Money Blocks Holding You Back," a friend of mine said this prayer. Four days later she received a $30,000 ghostwriting job! How awesome is that? If it can work for my friend, it can work for you, too!

Since writing my first book, *The Spiritual Path To Prosperity . . . The Truth About Money Revealed*, I have used this technique with many people, and they have all had amazing results. Here are some of their comments:

I'm not sure if you remember me. I reached out 3 months ago with some general advice and to express gratitude for an online session you'd provided. You prayed with me over a job interview I was to have later that afternoon, and I've been saying a version of that prayer ever since. Though I was selected for the position, I discovered the environment wasn't in alignment with the vision I have for sharing my services and talent, and I learned much from the process. My professional and financial situation aren't optimized at the moment, though today I am seeing more work coming my way, which gives me hope for the future :)

So, I want to express gratitude to you for that and for the prayer that has become a foundational part of my morning practice. I wish you well in the remains of 2020 and beyond.—J. H.

Dawn shared her manifestation technique with me and even took the time to make sure I understood how to customize it. When I say it aloud with conviction, it works every time. Sometimes it's not exactly what I expect, but it always delivers.—S. C.

I received an unexpected inheritance of $50k to help pay off some credit card debt.—D. W.

After Dawn did the manifestation prayer with me, I received $9,000 and may be up for a promotion.—K. A.

I was hoping to purchase a great home to retire in and tried the manifestation technique with Dawn a few months ago.

Sadly, I lost out to another bidder and was disappointed, of course. Dawn pointed out that it usually means something better will happen. Sure enough—2 months later a better opportunity came along—a nice home in a great neighborhood and $50,000 less. An offer was made and accepted and I was overjoyed that this happened after 2 years of searching. The manifestation technique Dawn helped me with worked! It takes time and faith . . . but it's worth it for sure. Try it!—J. D.

I am the person who needed a new car and was uncertain if the insurance company would even cover the water damage to my car. The situation is resolving itself very well. The amount paid by insurance is equal to the cost of my new car. God was absolutely involved in the outcome. Since the end of November, I have been renting a car, which costs over $450 per week due to the shortage of cars. I had planned to buy a jalopy that would last until the end of next year when the car market is expected to stabilize. However, God had something better planned.

I have learned to let friends and contacts know when I have a need. You never know who has a contact who may help you. Through a business contact of a friend, I was referred to a used car dealer in Manheim, Pennsylvania. When I looked at the dealer's website, I saw the exact car I ultimately wanted to buy in the color I was looking for, a metallic gray 2021 Mazda CX-5 Signature. When I saw it I knew it had to be from God because I had looked on the Mazda website and none were listed, new or used.

The personnel at the dealership were easy to deal with, and I bought the car. I told the salesperson I would have to return to pick up the Mazda, as I had a rental car that needed to be returned to Enterprise in Wayne, Pennsylvania. He told me, "There's an Enterprise location just down the road; see if you can return it there." I could for a small fee, so I did.

The next day—Saturday, January 8—my insurance company called to go over the payment. The payment equaled the cost of my Mazda. I was and am still so thankful for the resolution. God's power was definitely involved. I wanted you to know the resolution. Thank you for your prayer.—J. G.

I also shared my technique with a writer who was interviewing me for an article on my first book. She wanted to manifest money to pay for her son's college education. Four months later she called with an amazing story to share with me. Her son didn't get into his first-choice college, but he got into an even better school. The school had just instituted a policy that anyone in the ROTC program would get in-state tuition. Her son was in the ROTC program but would have been an out-of-state student. Out-of-state tuition was $52,000 a year, but in-state tuition was $13,000! Her son was getting four years of college for the price of what she would have paid for one year. She was thrilled. She thanked me again for sharing this technique with her.

The most amazing story I have heard from someone who used this technique was from a woman I met at a networking event. She owned a Philadelphia-area restaurant with her husband. Their chef had quit, and if they didn't find a new chef by the end of the month, they were going to have to close the restaurant. I approached her and asked if she was open to something a little outside of the box to help with her situation. She said, "Yes, what do I have to lose?"

I did the technique with her and didn't see her again until our next luncheon. I asked how she was doing and what had happened since we last met. She was so excited. What happened was a miracle, and it all transpired within two weeks of our previous meeting. Her husband was talking to a friend of his in Mexico who happened to know an award-winning chef. He gave her husband the chef's number. Turns out, the chef and his fiancée were traveling to New York City to get married in a week and a half. The chef's future wife was a pastry chef! Before the wedding, they interviewed the chef and his fiancée and hired them. They moved to the Philadelphia area, and the restaurant is thriving.

Even more, the chef and the woman from my networking group shared the same vision for the restaurant, and they were able to win over her husband, who had wanted to keep things the same. He thought she had put the chef up to talking to him about future plans for the restaurant, but she hadn't—it was synchronicity that she and the chef were on the same page. This woman manifested everything she wanted and more in such a short time. I was thrilled for her.

I use this technique to manifest everything in my life. I used it to manifest my first book, which became a bestseller on Amazon—#1 in the budgeting category and #2 in the investing and new thought categories. (The #1 book in new thought was Napoleon Hill's *Think and Grow Rich*. I was thrilled to be right behind the legendary Napoleon Hill.)

When people share their success stories with me, I feel the same exhilaration I do when I see my own manifestations. That's why I created my monthly Manifestation Power Hours. This monthly event is a group session where I conduct the manifestation technique with each person. I am available for individual manifestation sessions as well. Feel free to email me at dawnd516@gmail.com. Write "Manifestation Technique—Manifest & Invest" in the subject line when emailing me. Send me your success stories, too!

CHAPTER 5

Releasing the Five
Biggest Money Blocks

B efore I teach you about the different financial products and strategies used to accumulate wealth, it's important to clear any money blocks that are keeping you stuck in your current situation. Without clearing these blocks, it doesn't matter if you know how money works, because you won't be able to hold onto it long enough to use the strategies.

Take me as an example. I was making my clients money, and they were doing well. But I was unaware that I had subconscious money blocks that were holding me back from reaching my goals. Once I cleared them, money and business opportunities began flowing in unexpected ways.

Money is a tool for creating the life you want. People face many obstacles, and while some are external, many are related to internal money blocks that stand in the way of clarity and confidence. To move forward, you must shift your mindset and clear away things that keep you stuck in your present pattern. It doesn't matter whether you are single, married, divorced, widowed, retired, or working—taking control of your finances and finding the confidence to create transformation isn't just about moving money here or signing a form there.

If you focus exclusively on the nuts and bolts but neglect the internal issues—that is, your money blocks—you'll find yourself in the same place over and over again, overwhelmed and unsure. Wealth alone won't provide fulfillment or make you feel in control if your internal scripts are full of negativity and self-doubt. You might even re-accumulate debt after having worked your way out of it.

The good news is that once you clear the money blocks holding you back from reaching your financial goals, you can live the life you want. In addition to having more money, you will have confidence in your ability to make financial decisions. You will be able to talk about money openly with the right advisor so he or she can help you reach your goals faster. You will learn to prioritize your needs over others' needs—so you aren't, for example, jeopardizing your retirement to pay for your kid's college education. It doesn't have to be an either–or dilemma.

The five biggest money blocks people face are:[1]

1. Prioritizing others' needs over their own needs
2. Money secrecy
3. Lacking confidence in their own knowledge
4. Uncertainty and decision paralysis
5. Lacking trustworthy financial advice

Grab a notebook and pen, and let's take a look at how each one of these blocks can show up in your life.

I have created the following quiz to help you figure out which of the five money blocks are holding you back. Answer the quiz questions, then fill out the scoring guide. The five columns in the scoring guide represent the five money blocks. The highest-scoring column is your biggest money block. Read the corresponding section in Chapter 6 to find out how to release your biggest money blocks.

Money Block Quiz

What's holding you back? Take the quiz and find out.

1. I sometimes give more money than I can afford for weddings, birthdays, etc.
   A. Always
   B. Sometimes
   C. Seldom
   D. Never
   E. No way

2. I show my love by giving gifts of money.
   A. Always
   B. Sometimes
   C. Seldom
   D. Never
   E. No way

3. I don't like spending money on myself.
   A. Always
   B. Sometimes
   C. Seldom
   D. Never
   E. No way

4. I don't talk about how I spend my money.
   A. Always
   B. Sometimes
   C. Seldom
   D. Never
   E. No way

5. I dislike talking about money, salary, or other financial topics.
   A. Always
   B. Sometimes
   C. Seldom
   D. Never
   E. No way

6. I don't like talking to financial professionals because I don't feel heard.
   A. Always
   B. Sometimes
   C. Seldom
   D. Never
   E. No way

7. I'm afraid I'll ask stupid questions in conversations about money.
   A. Always
   B. Sometimes
   C. Seldom
   D. Never
   E. No way

8. I feel judged when I open up about money.
   A. Always
   B. Sometimes
   C. Seldom
   D. Never
   E. No way

9. I feel guilty about how I manage my money.
   A. Always
   B. Sometimes
   C. Seldom
   D. Never
   E. No way

10. I feel overwhelmed when I think about my finances.
    A. Always
    B. Sometimes
    C. Seldom
    D. Never
    E. No way

11. I know I need to make changes to my finances, but I don't know where to start.
    A. Always
    B. Sometimes
    C. Seldom
    D. Never
    E. No way

12. I'm not sure what my options are or what decisions I
    need to make.
    A. Always
    B. Sometimes
    C. Seldom
    D. Never
    E. No way

13. I don't have a trustworthy financial professional I can
    talk to about money.
    A. Always
    B. Sometimes
    C. Seldom
    D. Never
    E. No way

14. I don't think I have enough money to get professional
    advice.
    A. Always
    B. Sometimes
    C. Seldom
    D. Never
    E. No way

15. Markets are rigged, so I'd rather not do anything risky.
    A. Always
    B. Sometimes
    C. Seldom
    D. Never
    E. No way

Scoring
A = 20 points; B = 10 points; C = 5 points; D. = 2 points; E. = 0 points.

Record the point total for each quiz question in the corresponding numbered blank. Total each column. The highest total represents your biggest money block.

Block 1	Block 2	Block 3	Block 4	Block 5
1. _____	4. _____	7. _____	10. _____	13. _____
2. _____	5. _____	8. _____	11. _____	14. _____
3. _____	6. _____	9. _____	12. _____	15. _____
_____	_____	_____	_____	_____
Total	Total	Total	Total	Total

CHAPTER 6

What Money Block Do You Have?

Prioritizing Others' Needs over Your Own Needs

Do any of the following sound like you?

- I don't take time for myself because I don't want to be selfish.
- I sometimes give more money than I can afford for weddings, birthdays, and so forth.
- I show my love by giving gifts or money.
- I don't feel worthy unless I'm doing things for other people.
- Anything extra I have, I give to my kids or loved ones; they deserve it more than I do.
- I don't like spending money on myself.

If this sounds familiar, then prioritizing others' needs over your own is a block for you. These thoughts simply aren't true. The truth is, you must put on your own "oxygen mask" before helping others. Showing up for others as your best self starts with taking care of yourself.

Let's uncover the origin of this block. Write down your answers to the following questions, taking some time to reflect and be honest with yourself.

- What does this internal monologue tell you about your value to others?
- Where do these thoughts about yourself come from?
- What would it mean if you put yourself on an equal footing with others?

Now, let's replace this block with what you would like to believe instead.

For example, if you find it difficult to take time for yourself, tell yourself:

I value myself enough to be the first priority in my life. It's not about being selfish; it's about loving me in the best, healthiest way. It's about establishing boundaries and standing in my own power. When I do this, I am fulfilled. Being fulfilled enables me to give to others from a place of strength rather than weakness, because I feel that I have something, too.

Think of one small action you can take today to put yourself first. It could be as simple as sitting in your favorite chair outside with a cup of coffee and reading a book for however long you'd like. When we take care of ourselves first, we have more to give to others. When we take care of ourselves, others get the best version of us instead of a worn-out, depleted version!

Money Secrecy

Shh! Money secrecy is the next block. Your parents may have taught you that money is a private matter, that it's taboo to talk about money with others. Or maybe your parents never discussed money with you. Consequently, you stay quiet during money conversations, because you don't know what to say. You might find it hard to open up about money with your partner for fear of being judged. You might avoid talking about money with your siblings because you're afraid they will ask to borrow money from you if they know how much you have.

I never knew how much money my dad made, but I remember my mom saying, "If you find a guy half as good as your dad, you will be okay." As a little girl, I took that to mean the husband brings home the money, and the wife manages it. That doesn't work so well these days, when two incomes are often needed to provide for a family. Luckily, I was always ambitious and didn't accept the idea that a man was a financial plan. After reading this book, I hope you won't, either. It is so important for women to be financially independent, because life is unpredictable. Things can change in an instant. It's better to be prepared than sorry.

Here are some of the symptoms of a money secrecy block:

- I find it hard to open up about money with my partner or loved ones.
- I don't talk about how I spend my money.
- I stay quiet during conversations about money, because I don't know what to say.
- I dislike talking about money, salary, or other financial topics.
- I think money is a taboo topic.
- I don't like talking to financial professionals, because I don't feel heard.

- My partner and I are not on the same page about money.
- Money makes me anxious.

Ladies, did you know that staying silent about money contributes to lower salaries for women in the workplace? It also contributes to the common myth that women aren't as good with money as men.

In order to uncover these subconscious blocks and bring them into our conscious mind, it's important to write everything down. Once you write down your money blocks, they can be healed and released. So, write down your answers to the following questions:

- What is the first thing that pops into your head when you think about money?
- When did you start believing this?
- Where did this belief come from?

Now, ask yourself what you would like to believe instead. For example, if you are struggling to share your finances with your partner, tell yourself:

I am great at handling money. But by working with my partner, we can take advantage of both of our money-handling skill sets, and we will feel heard and valued by each other. We will know where we stand financially and be better able to make financial decisions together. We are on the same team, and we will reach our goals faster because we don't have any secrets. As a result, our relationship will improve.

You can take action today by opening up to your partner about your hesitation to discuss money. Baby steps go a long way. If you and your partner can talk openly about money, it will allow space for communication in other areas of your relationship as well.

Lacking Confidence in Your Own Knowledge

Are you overwhelmed when you think of your finances and goals? Do you think you should know more about money at this point in your life? Do you tell yourself you're just not good with numbers, and you'll never understand them? These are signs of Block #3, lacking confidence in your own knowledge.

Additional symptoms of this block include the following:
- I'm afraid I'll ask stupid questions.
- I feel intimidated when people use investment jargon.
- I feel judged when I open up about money.
- I don't feel heard by financial professionals.
- I feel guilty about how I manage my money.

It doesn't have to be this way. If you want to learn new things about money or learn how to handle your finances, reading this book is a good start! If you have some prior financial knowledge, this book can boost your confidence and confirm what you already know.

Let's get to the source of this block. Write down your answers to the following questions:
- Why do you believe these things?
- Where did this script come from?

What small step can you take today to counteract this block? To clear this block, simply replace it with what you would like to believe instead.

For example, if you have always believed you aren't good with numbers, tell yourself, "I am good with numbers, and I also have a calculator to verify."

Here's another step you can take. Tally all your current monthly expenses. Check how much money you have saved in your emergency fund. A rule of thumb is to aim for an emergency fund that covers six months of expenses if you have a single source of income or three months if you are a part of a two-income household, but you should always do what will make you feel secure if an emergency arises.

Uncertainty and Decision Paralysis

These days, uncertainty and decision paralysis are very common, because we're bombarded with information on a daily basis. You may suffer from this block if you find yourself saying the following:

- I know I need to make changes to my finances, but I don't know where to start.
- I went to talk to a financial professional, but I left even more confused.
- I'm not sure what my options are or what decisions I need to make.
- I feel overwhelmed when I think about my finances.
- I have to optimize every choice, or I'll fail.
- Retirement is so far away. I don't need to worry about it now.
- Retirement is so close that nothing I do will change anything.

The truth is you don't need to know all the answers before taking action. You can decide to start saving for retirement and then seek out a trusted professional to walk you through all the different options to find the best one for you.

Dig deeper into your internal monologue and answer the following questions. Write down everything that comes to mind, and don't censor yourself.

- When did you start believing these things?
- Where did it come from?

Now that you have gotten all those thoughts out of your system, let them go. Tell yourself:

If I don't have to be 100 percent correct about every decision, I can stop procrastinating. I can start saving and investing now. The more time I have to save and invest, the more time my money has to compound and grow. If I wait until some point in the future, I can never get my time back. I can find an advisor to put me on the right path and help me avoid costly mistakes. An advisor can simplify my finances for me. That's what they get paid for.

Today, you can take action by being conscious of your thoughts. Anytime a thought pops into your head that stops you from moving forward with your finances, pause and think about where it's coming from. Then, counteract the negative thought with a small action you can take to move forward in the right direction.

Lacking Trustworthy Financial Advice

This last block is a huge one. It *must* be overcome, because it will hold you back from reaching your goals and fulfilling your dreams. Research shows that working with a financial professional adds 3 percent to your bottom line.[1] Symptoms of this block are as follows:

- I don't think the financial industry is trustworthy.
- I feel bombarded by information, and it's all conflicting.
- I don't have anyone trustworthy to talk to about money.
- I don't think I have enough money to get professional advice.
- I'm not sure which source of information I can trust.
- Markets are rigged, so I'd rather not do anything risky.

Working with a professional is one of the smartest things you can do with your money. It is so much more than your portfolio. A professional is there to serve as your mentor, behavioral coach, and accountability partner.

Write down your answers to the following questions:

- If you believe any of the foregoing statements to be true, why do you feel that way?
- Where did these beliefs come from?
- Did you have a bad experience with financial advice in the past?

You can replace this block by being honest with yourself. What kind of advice do you need? If you're unsure, that's okay! Write down what you don't know.

What is one small action you can take today to counteract this block? You can call a financial professional to set up an interview. If there is synergy between the two of you, great; if not, keep calling financial professionals until you find one you are comfortable working with.

There are many other blocks around money, but these five are the most common. Write your answers to the following prompts for any other blocks you encounter:

- What beliefs do you hold about the block? Why?
- Where did these beliefs come from?
- What would you like to believe instead?
- What is one small step you can take to counteract the block?

If you do this whenever you encounter a block, your life will improve dramatically. You will be more fulfilled and have more abundance in your life!

CHAPTER 7

The Five Different Money Personality Types

Y ou have learned how to manifest and uncovered your money blocks; now it's time to learn your money personality type. When it comes to our financial wellness, we often neglect our money personality type—our approach and emotional response to money. We need to know ourselves and be in touch with our emotions in order to make the best financial decisions. All of us react to and feel differently about money.

The five different money personality types are:[1]

1. The compulsive moneymaker
2. The compulsive saver
3. The compulsive spender
4. Indifferent to money
5. The worrier

If you are a compulsive moneymaker, your priority is making more money. You believe making money is the key to happiness. You give your all to your work, often at the expense of personal relationships and experiences. You are likely to be the hardest-working person in the room. A compulsive moneymaker does the extra work to get ahead financially. If this describes you, consider stopping and smelling the roses once and a while. There is more to life than making money and, as the saying goes, you can't take it with you when you are dead and gone. Take a vacation or treat yourself to something you have always wanted.

The compulsive saver is like a squirrel trying to save as many nuts as it can. Saving makes you feel more secure, even if you don't have any of the things you are saving for or a plan for spending your money. Security doesn't come from having money. Yes, money helps, but true security comes from within. You need money to cover the basics, but beyond that, money doesn't give you the security you think it does. Money can't provide character, deep and meaningful relationships, or true friendships. These truly make us feel secure, and they begin with having a healthy sense of self-love. If you are a compulsive saver, don't let the fear of losing or spending money prevent you from enjoying what you have earned. You are usually the one friends turn to, because you how to find the best deals and you have the biggest emergency fund. Find a healthy balance between saving and spending. Moderation is the key. If you learn to balance saving and spending, you will have a more enjoyable life.

You know you are a compulsive spender if you spend money on things you don't need. Retail therapy is one of your favorite pastimes. You tend to be outgoing, and you treat yourself and others to the finer things in life. There doesn't need to be a special occasion. You are the life of the party and the best person to go shopping with. If you are not careful, you quickly find yourself in debt. Even if you already have substantial debts, you continue to shop. You may keep what you buy a secret from your spouse. Look inward and consider what makes you feel the need to buy things—especially for other people—in excess. Are you looking for love? Approval? Acceptance? Money can't buy those things. What you are seeking is within you. It's not out there in the world or in others. Create a spending plan and stick to it. That doesn't mean you can't spend your money—you just need to set money aside for things like retirement savings and your emergency fund before you start splurging. Don't carry credit card debt. If you can't pay off your credit card bill each month, you are overspending.

If you are indifferent to money, you don't stress or even think about money. You don't let money influence your decisions to do or not do things. One of your core beliefs is that money isn't the key to happiness. This is a healthy mindset to have, but if you ignore your finances, you may be headed for disaster. Many people rely on their spouse to handle the finances. I recommend you become involved. In unexpected circumstances, you may be forced to handle your finances. At the very least, learn what you have, why you have it, and where you can locate important documents. Get more comfortable with money. Know what the household expenses are, what your income is, and how much debt you have. This will save you a lot of financial stress in the future.

The last of the five money personalities is the worrier. The worrier is constantly fretting about losing everything, no matter how much money they have. If you are a worrier, you always plan for the worst-case scenario. This is unhealthy; it keeps you stuck in scarcity mode. You let fear stand in your way of enjoying life and taking advantage of opportunities to increase your wealth. It is great to prepare for the future, but worriers go overboard in their anxiety. If you are a worrier, look inward to discover where your fears originate. The tools in this book can help you overcome your fears. You may need to talk to a therapist to work through this issue. Take baby steps. Believe in yourself and educate yourself on money—your confidence will grow, and your worries will shrink.

You probably fit into more than one of the money personality types. Most of us are a combination of multiple types. There are no good or bad types, so don't shame yourself. The only way to improve your financial well-being is to know your strengths and weaknesses and how to work on them.

Part 2
How to Save

CHAPTER 8

What Makes Me Qualified to Give Financial Advice?

———

What makes me qualified to give financial advice? In addition to walking the walk from poverty to six figures, I went to Adelphi University and received my Bachelor of Science in finance. When I went into the financial services industry, I had to pass a series of tests. I quit my job and moved to Scranton, Pennsylvania, the Friday before I took my first test. If I hadn't passed the test that Monday, I would have been unemployed for 30 days. Fortunately, I passed the test. During my first year in the business, I also earned my first professional designation, Life Underwriter Training Council Fellow (LUTCF). This required passing five classes from the American College of Financial Services.

Years later I wanted to take my practice to the next level, so I enrolled in the CERTIFIED FINANCIAL PLANNER™ program. This was no easy task. I took the self-study route. I had to take six classes (including tax, insurance, financial planning, retirement planning, investments, and estate planning), present a financial plan to a professor assigned to evaluate me, secure a recommendation from someone who was already a CFP®, and have at least three years of planning experience.

At the conclusion of each course, I had to pass a proctored final exam before I could move on to the next course. I passed each exam on my first try until I got to the investments class. When I enrolled, I psyched myself out. The person who registered me said he dropped out of the class because it was so difficult. I ended up quitting halfway through because it *was* difficult, and I was afraid I would fail the exam.

That ended up being a three-year break. But I'm not a quitter. I wanted to finish what I started, so I completed my last two courses in one year, then went straight into the Capstone class, where I had to create a financial plan. I scheduled the CFP® exam for later that year. I was concerned because the exam covers all six classes and there had been a three-year gap in my studies. However, thanks to a review class, I am proud to say I passed my CFP® exam on my first attempt. It was the hardest test I have ever taken in my life! The questions are tricky, so you have to know your stuff inside and out. My heart was pounding when I hit "Enter" to see my results. Seeing "Passed" made me so happy! I couldn't believe it. I was shaking. Only 62 percent pass on their first try.

As a CFP® professional, it is my mission to teach people the truth about how money really works so they can reach their financial goals with peace of mind. I also want to inspire people with economic confidence.

This year, I became a member of Ed Slott's Elite IRA Advisor Group[SM]. There are only 450 members in the country. Ed Slott's website[1] says:

Members of Ed Slott's Elite IRA Advisor Group℠ train with Ed Slott and his team of IRA Experts on a continuous basis. These advisors pass regular background checks, complete requisite training, attend semiannual workshops, webinars, and complete mandatory exams. They are immediately notified of changes to the tax code and updates on retirement planning, so you can be sure your retirement dollars are safe from unnecessary taxes and fees. Additionally, members have access to us, America's IRA Experts to answer any tough questions or planning needs.

Let's face it. Money is a confusing topic for many people. There is a lot of stress and anxiety around money, which sometimes leaves people feeling overwhelmed. I am passionate about educating people on how to invest for the long term. My mission in life is to help people by showing them the truth about money and cutting through all the noise around growing your money over the long haul.

I love helping people manage their money and reach their goals by providing them with information that is clear and easy to digest. Many people struggle to find the clarity and confidence they need to take action when it comes to their money. Some lack confidence in their knowledge. Some are overwhelmed by information and decisions. Others are too busy to deal with handling their money and simply want assurance that they are using proven, real-world investment strategies.

When you let go of fear and change your beliefs about money, your level of clarity and confidence will change, too. Once you clear your money blocks, you can take advantage of time-tested investment strategies to make the most of your money. Having a written financial plan and someone like me to help you avoid costly mistakes will improve your financial situation—current and future.

In order to fulfill your destiny, you need to get your financial house in order and understand how money works. I've written this book to help you do just that. This book will help you remove spiritual blocks around money so you can step into a life without debt, retire sooner than you ever thought was possible, and accumulate wealth so you can live out your dreams. I'll teach you how to grow your money without complicated strategies or big sacrifices in your day-to-day life. If you want your money to work harder so you don't have to, keep reading!

CHAPTER 9:

Women and Money

Money is a particularly intimidating topic for many women, so I am dedicating this entire chapter to demystifying your finances. We will cover three truths about your money:

1. You and your finances come first.
2. Money management is a skill, not an inherited trait.
3. Tend and befriend your money.

We will also cover two money myths:[1]

1. It's better to defer money management to men.
2. You can be creative or good with numbers, but not both.

If you are ready to take control of your money and put a strategy in place that works for you, then keep reading. The basics of money management are simple.

Are you interested in taking control of your money, but you find yourself remaining silent while men talk about money (possibly yours), worried that you will sound stupid if you speak up?

Do you watch the news and wish you knew more about what they are talking about, but you find the financial world intimidating and complex?

Are you afraid of being scammed out of your life savings?

You are great at what you do in your career, as a mother, or in your hobbies, but you feel like you don't have control of your finances. You let your husband deal with the money so there will be one less thing to deal with—and that doesn't feel right. You don't want to reach retirement and look back, thinking, "If I had learned how to handle my finances and gotten help sooner, I wouldn't have to work at Walmart in my golden years."

The good news is you can start turning things around today. Money isn't as complicated as it seems. You can take back control of your finances.

You need to know how to handle your finances yourself, whether you are single, married, divorced, or widowed. If you let someone else in your household handle the money, what happens when they are no longer in the picture? You may get divorced. The person handling the money may die or become disabled and no longer be able to manage the money.

I had a very successful prospect cancel a financial plan that included guaranteed retirement income for the rest of her life and a well-balanced portfolio of investments because her boyfriend thought it was a bad idea. It was her money and *she* was supporting *him*, yet she wouldn't make financial decisions that benefited her without her boyfriend's approval. He wasn't even her husband. I don't want any smart women reading this to be in the same situation.

No one was born knowing how to manage money. Everyone who knows how to manage money had to *learn*—and you can learn, too. Start building your financial muscles so you can have a healthy financial life. In the following sections, we will cover some truths and myths about money. I will also give you some questions to ask yourself. All of the questions in this chapter are great to discuss with yourself.

Money Truth: You and Your Finances Should Come First

Our society encourages women to take care of everyone else before themselves. Many women sacrifice everything for their children. Some do so because they want to give their kids the life they never had. This practice is sometimes unhealthy and may be detrimental to your finances. Your children would much rather have you be financially independent than have to support you in retirement. When you take care of your finances, you set a good example of how important it is to save for retirement and not spend everything you make. This is not selfish. Putting you first is smart. If you are feeling stuck and can't move forward, ask yourself:

- Am I currently putting someone else's finances before mine?
- What happens if I run out of money because other people come first?
- Do I have a way to save money for my financial future?
- What is my plan for my senior years?
- Have I had a trustworthy financial professional review my plan?

Money Truth: Money Management Is a Skill, Not an Inherited Trait

You can spend hours looking at different investment strategies and reading as many personal finance books as you can—but you don't have the time, and it's not necessary. Money management doesn't have to be complicated. There are plenty of tried-and-true strategies that will help you create a solid financial footing for you and your family. You will find many of these strategies in this book.

There are four basic things you need to know when it comes to money:

1. Income: How much is coming in?
2. Expenses: How much is going out?
3. Assets: How much do you own?
4. Debts: How much do you owe?

The more income you have left over after meeting your expenses, the more you can save for the future and/or use to pay off debt. It's that simple. You may need help with strategies to increase income, reduce expenses, get out of debt faster, and invest. Ask yourself these questions:

- Do I have a good understanding of the four money management pillars?
- If not, which one(s) do I need to learn more about?
- Am I confident in my ability to learn what I need to know?
- Is there a trusted financial professional I can reach out to for advice and guidance?

Money Truth: Tend and Befriend Your Money

One way you can befriend your money is to schedule "money dates" once a month. Look at your spending plan and see if any adjustments need to be made for the next month. For any big expenses, like being in a friend's wedding, make sure you plan ahead by setting money aside for that goal as soon as you find out.

Having people you can talk to about your money is critical to building your savings. People who are experienced with money can speed up your learning curve, and talking to a professional can help you avoid costly mistakes. Soliciting sound advice will increase your confidence in your ability to manage your money. Everyone's situation is unique, so make sure the professional you work with listens to your fears and concerns without dismissing or ignoring them. Here are some questions you should ask yourself:

- How confident do I feel about handling my own finances?
- Do I know someone who can help me work with my money?
- Am I confident that my partner can listen and advise?
- Is there a financial professional who can apply their knowledge of finances to my specific financial situation?

Money Myth: It's Better to Defer Money Management to the Men

Have you ever been at a social event talking about finances, and the men are doing all the talking, boasting about their latest, greatest investments? Do you exit the conversation to avoid all the hot air? You may have thought that much of the content of the conversation was wrong, but you didn't want to interject the truth or voice your opinion. Many women feel this way, because we were taught to be nice and not interrupt. Has your advisor ignored you and spoken directly to your husband while you were sitting right there? Your voice deserves to be heard and recognized.

Your goals and priorities must be front and center. It doesn't matter if you don't have the same priorities as others. Once you clear away all the noise, you can gain clarity on your financial goals. Then, you can create a roadmap to achieve them. Ask yourself these questions:

- Do I have a firm grasp of my financial priorities?
- Can I see my way clear to creating a money strategy that works for me?
- What would a workable financial roadmap for me and my family look like?
- Am I connected to a financial professional who can help me achieve both clarity and my money goals?

Money Myth: You Can Be Creative or Good with Numbers, but Not Both

Left-brained people are good with logic and numbers. Right-brained people are creative and spontaneous. Science actually proves this isn't true.[2]

I definitely use both sides of my brain. How else would I write a book like this? You probably already know people in your life who are good at numbers and have a creative side, too. Mathematicians are often musicians or artists.

If you are still not convinced that you will ever be good at numbers, the good news is that you really don't have to be. We live in an age where there is an app for everything. You can track your spending with an app. There is software that will show you how much you need to save to reach a particular goal and what investments are appropriate for your risk tolerance. And you can always turn to a financial professional, because they have more knowledge and can custom-tailor plans to your individual needs. Here are some questions to ask yourself:

- Am I convinced that I'll never be good with numbers?
- Do I think of myself as only artistic and/or creative?
- Are there tools that can help me with money management?
- Do I have a trustworthy financial professional who can guide me through all the numbers?

What are you waiting for? Flex your money muscles and fall in love with your financial power! The best time to plant a tree is 20 years ago; the second-best time is now. The same holds true for managing your money.

It's important for women to take the driver's seat for their own financial strategy. There will be times when you don't have someone else to rely on. Knowing the basics will help you determine who you can trust when you decide to get financial advice. Money isn't something only men can handle. It's a tool for you to be able to have the life you want, now and in the future.

CHAPTER 10

Saving Money Made Easy

M any people think that if they earn more money, they will be financially stable. That is simply not true.

Do you save the raises you receive each year? If you do, then I congratulate you! That is a great step toward financial stability.

The problem most of us have is that, when we *make* more money, we *spend* more money. That does not provide financial stability or help us build wealth. Even if you make six or seven figures a year, you can still be broke!

It doesn't have to be this way. You can start saving early instead of spending everything you make. That is the difference between *building* wealth and giving off the *appearance* of being wealthy.

No matter your income level, you can have financial stability. The way is simple: Live below your means. Don't spend everything you make. Pay down credit card debt, build an emergency fund, stick to a financial plan, save for retirement, and protect your earnings with life and disability insurance. With every paycheck, pay yourself first. No matter what stage of life you are in, you can be financially secure.

The first step toward financial stability is to know where you stand. If you don't know where you are, it's hard to reach your destination. Take an inventory of your assets, income, and expenses. If you find that you have more expenses than income, it's time to start reevaluating your priorities and choices.

Ideally, you should save 20 percent of your income. If that is not possible, start with 10 percent and work your way up to 20 percent. Every time you receive a paycheck, save 20 percent before you spend the rest. In other words, pay yourself first. If you are saving 5 percent in a retirement plan through your job, then you can save 15 percent, although I still recommend 20 percent if possible. The 20 percent goes toward building your emergency fund and meeting your short- and long-term goals, such as retirement. After you have put 20 percent in savings, you have 80 percent left to live on. You can make it work. Making it work might mean you eat out once a week instead of twice.

Some people want more structure in their spending plan. A popular spending plan is the 50/30/20 plan. In this plan, 50 percent is spent on needs, that is, anything you need to live and survive. This includes:

- Housing
- Medical expenses
- Utilities (the essentials like gas and electricity)
- Groceries

The next 30 percent goes to wants, the extras in life that make you happy. This includes:

- Dining out

- Cell phone bills
- Pets
- Internet
- Subscription services
- Shopping
- Entertainment
- Vacations
- Gifting and charitable donations
- Luxury car purchases (versus a basic car to get you from point A to point B)

The final 20 percent goes to short- and long-term debt repayment and savings. Depending on where you live and what you make, you may have to adjust these numbers slightly.

If you like more detailed plans, you can use the zero-sum spending plan. The zero-sum plan is good for people who earn a living on commissions or have irregular income. It requires you to think about every dollar you spend. Using last month's income, assign each dollar to this month's expenses. Give every dollar a *job* to prevent waste, maximize the use of your income, and reach the ultimate goal of zero overspending at the end of the month. You should have one month of expenses saved before you start using this method. If you have excess, you still assign it somewhere—for example, make an extra debt payment or put extra money into savings. If you don't assign the excess, it is usually wasted. If your income fluctuates, assign money using your lowest income month or the average for each category over the last twelve months.

As you are considering which spending plan to use, remember that it's important to pick a plan that will work for you. If you are debt free except for your mortgage and want a simple plan, saving 20 percent and living on 80 percent is a good choice. If you have a lot of debt and need to curb wasteful spending to get your finances on track, the zero-sum spending plan may work best for you. If you are still operating with a scarcity mindset and have a hard time spending money for your wants, the 50/30/20 plan may work for you. I hope you will use the abundance prayer and clearing your money blocks so the scarcity mindset isn't a problem for long. The bottom line is to implement one of these spending plans and stick with it so you can achieve financial stability.

Sometimes we are lucky enough to get a bonus, a gift, or an unexpected windfall. What should you do with it? Spend half and save the other half. If you are carrying debt, use the half that you spend to pay it off. If the windfall isn't enough to eliminate your debt, then use 25 percent to pay down the debt and spend 25 percent. We will talk more about how to eliminate debt in the next chapter.

CHAPTER 11:

Getting and Staying Out of Debt

A nyone can end up in debt, wealthy or not. There are many reasons why people accumulate debts: divorce, unforeseen medical expenses, or the sudden death of a spouse who didn't have enough life insurance.

Many debts are precipitated by events that you can't control. Buying the proper amount of insurance *is* within your control, but many people are blocked when it comes to buying insurance. I want to focus on the reasons we go into debt that *are* within our control. Unless we uncover the reasons we are in debt and face these demons, we will accrue debts over and over again. It's best to deal with *why* we are in debt before we get into the process of getting out of debt.

Why Am I in Debt?

Suppose you grew up poor and were told you couldn't have something, because it wasn't affordable. When you grew up and got a job, you wanted to spoil yourself because you had sacrificed and now you want the things you couldn't have when you were younger.

Or, perhaps you want to appear successful to others so they will approve of you. So, you buy things to keep up with the Joneses. Soon enough, you are thousands of dollars in debt and feel worse than you did before you bought all that stuff.

In both of these scenarios, you created debt to fill an internal void. *Stuff* won't make you happy. We find true happiness *within*. Clearing our blocks and facing our shadows and demons sets us on the path to being debt free.

I'm in the financial planning profession; I graduated at the top of my class. Yet I have made poor choices with my money that landed me in debt. At some point, we all make bad decisions with our money. I went into debt in the name of love (that is, because I wanted a particular person to love me). I'm smart enough to know that money can't buy love. But because I didn't love myself in the healthiest and best way, I ended up making decisions based on emotions rather than reason. This kind of thing can happen to anyone.

I was 21 and in love with a guy who was 36. He told me a sob story about how he had lost faith in love since his divorce, and he believed he would never love again. I set out on a mission to make him love me and prove to him that love exists. He definitely was not worthy of my love. It was an emotionally abusive relationship, to say the least, and I became his sugar mama.

Needless to say, I spent all my money on him and let him have free rein with my credit card. After I finally smartened up a few years later and had suffered enough, I was $36,000 in debt! My parents offered to pay off my debts and put me through school to get a master's degree in education. At the time, I couldn't see their generosity. I thought they were trying to control me and run my life, and my stubbornness and pride would not allow that. I didn't want to be a teacher! I was going to be a star! Besides, I had a finance degree as my backup plan. I also believed I had to punish myself. Because I had gotten myself into that mess, I had to get myself out of it.

And that is what I did. I had a salary of only $26,000 at the time, so I bartended every Friday and Saturday until 4:00 a.m. for a year straight. It was hard work, but I was determined, and I was debt free in a year. Every extra penny I made went to repaying my debt. I was so proud of myself.

We are all human, and money is an emotional subject. No woman should have to experience what I went through, so I want you to know that you are enough and perfect the way you are. The love you may be seeking in someone else is already inside of you. Meditate on and connect with that truth, and you will be truly happy.

Methods to Eliminate Debt

There are two methods to reduce debt:
1. The snowball method
2. The avalanche method

As we are considering which method will work for you, have your list of expenses (from when you created your spending plan) handy. List of each credit card with its balance, interest rate, and minimum payment. Figure 1 illustrates what your list might look like.

	Balance	Interest Rate	Minimum Monthly Payment
Chase Card	$945.00	14.5%	$20.00
Discover Card	$3000.00	9.9%	$50.00
Mastercard	$4600.00	12.9%	$75.00

Figure 1

If you want to prioritize paying off one card at a time instead of reducing overall debt as quickly as possible, the snowball method is best for you. It works like this:

1. Arrange your cards from smallest balance to largest balance.
2. Figure out how much extra money you can pay (in addition to the minimum payments).
3. Use the extra money to pay off the card with the smallest balance (the first one on your list.)
4. Make the minimum payment on the rest of the cards.
5. When the first card is paid off, use the extra money to pay off the card with the next-lowest balance.
6. Repeat this procedure until all your credit cards are paid off.

Figure 2 shows the timeline of payments for a person who has $500 a month to pay down the debts in Figure 2.

Figure 2: Debt Snowball Method

#	Month	Chase Card	Discover Card	Mastercard	Snowball Amt.	Add'l Payments	Total Interest	Balance	Total Payments
1	Feb 2023	$375	$50	$75	$355		$86	$8,545	$500
2	Mar 2023	$375	$50	$75	$355		$81	$8,131	$500
3	Apr 2023	$213	$212	$75	$355		$76	$7,711	$500
4	May 2023		$425	$75	$375		$71	$7,285	$500
5	Jun 2023		$425	$75	$375		$68	$6,856	$500
6	Jul 2023		$425	$75	$375		$64	$6,424	$500
7	Aug 2023		$425	$75	$375		$61	$5,988	$500
8	Sep 2023		$425	$75	$375		$57	$5,548	$500
9	Oct 2023		$425	$75	$375		$53	$5,105	$500
10	Nov 2023		$298	$202	$375		$49	$4,658	$500
11	Dec 2023			$500	$425		$45	$4,205	$500
12	Jan 2024			$500	$425		$40	$3,750	$500
13	Feb 2024			$500	$425		$35	$3,291	$500
14	Mar 2024			$500	$425		$30	$2,826	$500
15	Apr 2024			$500	$425		$25	$2,357	$500
16	May 2024			$500	$425		$20	$1,882	$500
17	Jun 2024			$500	$425		$15	$1,402	$500
18	Jul 2024			$500	$425		$10	$917	$500
19	Aug 2024			$427	$352		$5	$427	$427

Figure 2[1]

By using the snowball method, the total principal and interest paid is $9,437. The total interest paid is $892. The percentage paid in interest is 9.46 percent. You would be debt free in 1.6 years (19 months) rather than the 8.2 years it would take if you made only the minimum payments. Using the snowball method, you are debt free 6.8 years sooner!

The other method to pay down debt is the avalanche method. In this method, you pay off the card with the highest interest rate first. You pay less interest with this method, but as you will see in the example, the difference is minimal.

1. Arrange your credit cards from highest to lowest interest rate. Don't worry about the balances.

2. Figure out how much extra money you can pay in addition to the minimum payments.

3. Use the extra money to pay off the card with the highest interest rate (the first card on your list).

4. Make the minimum payment on the cards with lower interest rates.
5. When the first card is paid off, use the extra money to pay off the card with the next-highest interest rate.
6. Repeat this procedure until all your credit cards are paid off.

Figure 3 shows the timeline of payments for a person who has $500 a month to pay down this debt. In this case, Chase happens to have the highest interest rate and lowest balance.

Debt Avalanche-pay highest interest rate first

#	Month	Chase Card	Mastercard	Discover Card	Snowball Amt.	Add'l Payments	Total Interest	Balance	Total Payments
1	Feb 2023	$375	$75	$50	$355		$86	$8,545	$500
2	Mar 2023	$375	$75	$50	$355		$81	$8,131	$500
3	Apr 2023	$213	$237	$50	$355		$76	$7,711	$500
4	May 2023		$450	$50	$375		$71	$7,285	$500
5	Jun 2023		$450	$50	$375		$66	$6,856	$500
6	Jul 2023		$450	$50	$375		$62	$6,422	$500
7	Aug 2023		$450	$50	$375		$57	$5,984	$500
8	Sep 2023		$450	$50	$375		$53	$5,541	$500
9	Oct 2023		$450	$50	$375		$48	$5,094	$500
10	Nov 2023		$450	$50	$375		$43	$4,641	$500
11	Dec 2023		$450	$50	$375		$38	$4,184	$500
12	Jan 2024		$450	$50	$375		$33	$3,723	$500
13	Feb 2024		$450	$50	$375		$28	$3,256	$500
14	Mar 2024		$129	$371	$375		$23	$2,784	$500
15	Apr 2024			$500	$450		$19	$2,306	$500
16	May 2024			$500	$450		$15	$1,825	$500
17	Jun 2024			$500	$450		$11	$1,340	$500
18	Jul 2024			$500	$450		$7	$851	$500
19	Aug 2024			$358	$308		$3	$358	$358

Figure 3[2]

By following the avalanche method, the total principal and interest paid is $9,365. The total interest paid is $820, and the percentage paid in interest is 8.76 percent. You would be debt free in 1.4 years (17 months) compared to the 8.2 years it would take if you made only the minimum payments.

Using the avalanche method, you will be debt free in the same amount of time, but you will pay less interest. It's not a huge difference. The amount you save will depend on your particular debts.

Both methods work if you stay consistent, but the snowball method may work better for you if you judge success by having cards completely paid off—even if it means paying a little more in interest as you get out of debt.

No matter which method you use, if you slip up and miss a payment, get back on track as fast as you can. The more consistent you are with your payments, the faster your snowball or avalanche will eliminate your debts.

Once you are out of debt, make sure you don't rack up credit card debts again. Only buy what you can afford to pay off in full each month. Or better yet, pay cash and keep yourself out of debt, period. You will be glad you did!

Part 3

What to Do Once You Have Money

CHAPTER 12

How to Invest in the Stock Market

nvesting in the stock market doesn't have to be complicated,
although the financial services industry doesn't want you to
know this. The industry continually develops complicated
strategies and packages them as the latest, greatest product you
need in order to reach your goals. I believe many industry professionals develop these strategies for job security. Although these
complicated strategies may be good for some—like the super
wealthy—most people just need a simple, proven strategy to reach
their financial goals.

Because the strategy I will teach you in this chapter is simple,
you may think your advisor is not doing much to earn their fee.
But that is far from the truth! If you believe your advisor needs to
constantly buy and sell trying to beat the market or you question
whether your advisor is worth their fee, you may have a block in
this area. Follow the steps in Chapter 5 to clear the block and stop
limiting your ability to reach your goals.

Evidence-Based Investing

Let me ask you a question. Do you want to (1) gamble with your retirement money and take unnecessary risks based on your gut feelings or the advice of a so-called expert, or would you rather (2) use a simple, proven strategy that takes the guesswork out of investing for retirement and future goals?

Right, I'm going with the second option as well.

I believe in the evidence-based investing philosophy. Evidence clears the path to investing success and shows us which risks are not worth taking. Evidence has positively impacted results in nearly every aspect of our lives. What does evidence do? It supports theory.

For many years, people thought the earth was flat. The popular opinion was that you could fall off the edge of the earth—until it was proven through scientific evidence that the earth is, in fact, round. The idea that the earth is flat sounds ridiculous today, but we are not so different from historic flat-earthers. Once we have adopted a thought or belief, we hold onto it until it's proven otherwise. When science progresses, we see the truth and change our beliefs.

Consider evidence in medicine. When I was a kid, we didn't wear helmets while riding our bikes. But today, no parent would dare let their child ride a bike without a helmet. Why? Did my parents love me less than today's parents love their children? Of course not! The Bicycle Safety Institute reports that almost three-quarters of fatal bike crashes (74 percent) involve a head injury.[1] Nearly all bicyclists who die in accidents (97 percent) are not wearing a helmet. With this evidence, it is clear that riding a bike without a helmet isn't safe.

DNA evidence has changed the way crimes are solved. Before the late 1980s, there was no DNA testing, so detectives solved cases based on hunches. Can you imagine how many innocent people were wrongfully accused? I would never want to be accused of a crime—especially not in the days before DNA testing! Once DNA testing became available, cold cases were reopened and solved and innocent people were freed after years of being locked up for crimes they didn't commit. *Evidence* reveals the truth about a situation.

Without evidence, investors are lured into harmful investment decisions. Most investors don't make investment decisions based on evidence; they make decisions based on *emotions*. They try to time the market, pick individual stocks, chase manager performance, and manage their own portfolio.

Market Timing

Market timing is the practice of moving in and out of the market or switching between asset classes based on predictive methods. Many technical analysts rely on charts and look for the support and resistance levels. Once the market goes above or below a certain level, they make a move with their portfolio. In order to earn money this way, an investor has to know when the market has hit the bottom and when it's hit its peak.

The cover of the March 9, 2009, edition of *Time Magazine* had a photo of hands clenching a breaking rope.[2] The headline read, "Holding on for Dear Life." If you saw that cover as you waited in the supermarket checkout line, you might have thought, "Oh no, this isn't looking good! The market is going to keep dropping. I better move my investments to cash and wait until things get better." If you had acted based on that cover, you would have been very disappointed. The day that issue came out marked the bottom of the market and the beginning of the recovery from the financial crisis. The stock market rose from that point.

History repeated itself on March 23, 2020. The stock market was at a low. Again, many people panicked and moved to cash, and they missed out on a stock market rebound and record highs. If you knew on January 1, 2020, that a pandemic and social and political unrest were coming, you probably would not have predicted record stock market highs later in the year. You most likely would have assumed the market was going crash and stay down.

Of course, not all investors think this way. For every seller, there is a buyer. As billionaire investor Warren Buffett once said, "Buy when there is blood in the streets." When you see a good stock at garage sale prices, that is the time to buy, not sell.

So, is there evidence for buying more when the market is down—or at least not selling at that time? Figure 4 shows what would have happened if you had $100,000 invested in certain index funds from September 2008 to December 2019.

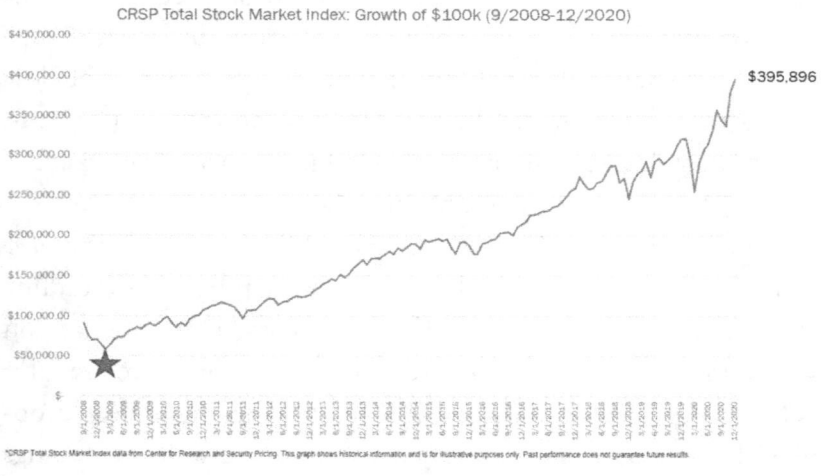

Figure 4[3]

In 1990, William F. Sharpe, a professor of finance at Stanford University, was awarded the Nobel Prize for Economics for his work in developing models to help with investment decisions. In 1975, he published an article titled "Likely Gains from Market Timing"[5] that proved that a trader would have to guess right 74 percent of the time to benefit from a market timing strategy.

Figure 5 summarizes what would have happened if you had $10,000 invested in 1980 and remained fully invested until 2018. You would have more than tripled your initial investment. However, if you tried to time the market, you would have experienced much less growth and may have had negative returns. That's because you have to be right 74 percent of the time to earn money timing the market. I don't like those odds!

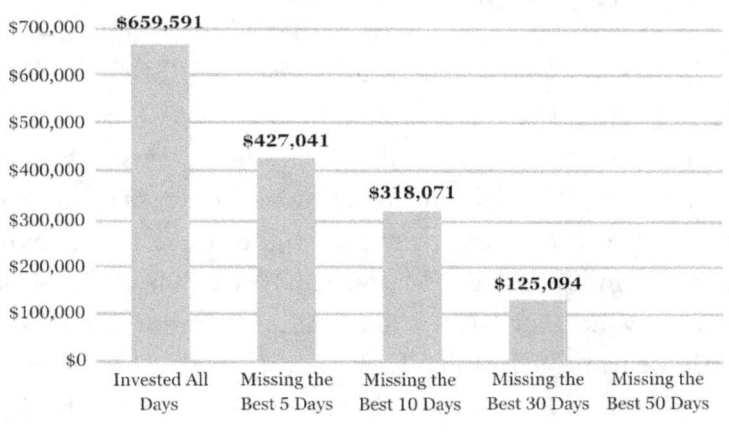

Missing the Best Days

Initial investment of $10,000 in the S&P 500 invested form 1980 - 2018

Data from Fidelity

Figure 5[4]

Picking Individual Stocks

Some people dream of striking it rich by picking stocks. They hear how others have made millions picking stocks, and they want in on it. If that's your dream, I'm sorry to burst your bubble—it's not a winning strategy for your hard-earned money or a pathway to successfully reaching your goals. Being successful with stock picking has a lot in common with winning the lottery. There is more luck than skill involved, and the chances are extremely slim that you will be correct over the long term.

Investors aren't alone in this line of thinking, though. Many advisors also attempt to build portfolios with individual stocks based on predictive measures. Let's look at how financial experts from a few money magazines did in 2016. They each had a "best stocks" list. If you followed the list from *MSN* or *Investor Place*, you would have earned 2.3 percent that year. *Kiplinger's* list earned 3.7 percent. The stock picks from *Time* and *Money Magazine* (which isn't even around anymore) earned 4.9 percent. *Barron's* had the best-performing picks, earning 5.3 percent. Now, compare that to what you would have earned if you simply invested in the Center for Research in Security Prices (CRSP) Total Stock Market Index—a whopping 12.83 percent![7]

There is a game I like to play at my live events. I fill up a Mason jar with 500 jellybeans to represent the stocks of the S&P 500 index. Every year, approximately 300 of these stocks underperform the index.[8] In the Mason jar, I mix 300 BeanBoozled jellybeans—which have flavors like toothpaste and stinky socks—with 200 delicious jellybeans. I ask for volunteers to see who can pick a good one. Some get lucky, but about 60 percent of the time, they end up spitting out the jellybean.

When I first picked one, I got a really nasty jellybean—I think the flavor was dog food. It was so gross I had to spit it out, wash my mouth out, and drink something. At least that wasn't a mistake I made with my hard-earned money! Picking a tasty jellybean is like picking a winning stock—except when you make a bad stock pick, you suffer more than a bad taste in your mouth.

If you need another reason to avoid investing in individual stocks, let's not forget about some of the biggest bankruptcies in history: Enron, CIT (a bank holding company), GM, World Com, Washington Mutual, and Lehman Brothers. These were all solid companies at one point, but they ended up losing billions and went bankrupt. No one could have predicted this would happen to such successful companies. Once again, the evidence shows that we shouldn't try to pick stocks.

Jack Bogle, founder of the Vanguard Group, once said, "Don't look for the needle in the haystack. Just buy the haystack."[9] In other words, buy the whole market, not individual stocks.

Chasing Manager Performance

At this point, you might be thinking, "I know I can't time the markets or pick individual stocks, but I can find people who can." I'm happy that you understand the first part, but I'm going to have to burst your bubble once again. Past performance is no guarantee of future results. Investors hear this time and time again, but they don't believe it! Regardless, it's true—that's why it's required on every piece of financial literature.

Here is a perfect example. In August 2006, Bill Miller, Legg Mason's fund manager, was touted by *Smart Money Magazine* as one of the "World's Greatest Investors."[10] During the financial crisis in 2008, he snapped up AIG, Wachovia, Bear Stearns, and Freddie Mac. The latter three nearly collapsed, and Miller rode them all the way down. Even the best money manager couldn't replicate his success.

Figure 6 shows that very few money managers can repeat the previous year's performance in the second year. In 2007 and 2008, no money managers did.

How many managers repeat their performance?

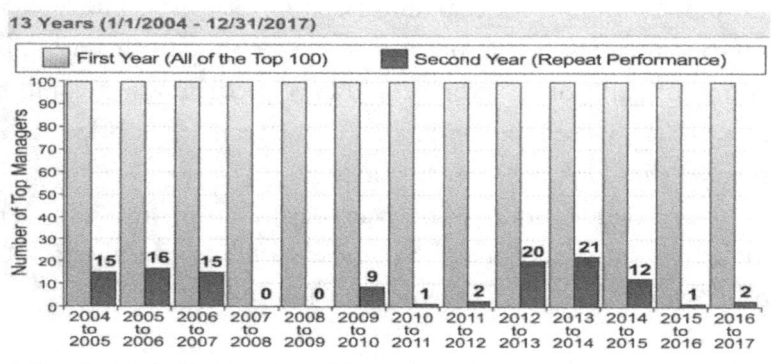

Figure 6[5]

Many people make investment decisions based on what forecasters (the talking heads on TV) say. But they are often wrong, and following their advice can destroy wealth. In a *Fortune* magazine article entitled, "Confessions of a Mutual Fund Reporter," an anonymous author wrote:

By day we write "Six Funds to Buy NOW!" ... By night, however, we invest in sensible index funds. .... Unfortunately, rational, pro-index-fund stories don't sell magazines, cause hits on Websites [sic], or boost Nielsen ratings. So rest assured: You'll keep on seeing those enticing but worthless SIX FUNDS TO BUY NOW! headlines as long as there are personal-finance media.[12]

Wow! Evidence straight from the source. As you can see, chasing a manager's past performance does not guarantee success.

Managing Your Own Portfolio

The best way to reach your financial goals with peace of mind is to follow the evidence-based investing philosophy and work with a CFP® professional. The biggest impact financial advisors have is to prevent you from making emotional decisions that could cost you thousands of dollars or more. Yes, you can open up an e-trade account or use a robo-advisor to invest on your own, but that only works if you know exactly what you are doing.

As I mentioned previously, working with a CFP® professional adds 3 percent to your bottom line. There are some strategies that only qualified advisors can help you with, such as using your home to provide tax-free retirement income or using the tax code to help you with your cash flow.

Having an advisor to call benefits you, because you have a relationship with your advisor. They know you and your goals, and they have an interest in your well-being. You can open up to them about your situation. The more information your advisor has, the more they can help you.

Using a robo-advisor takes the human element out of financial planning. A robo-advisor only focuses on numbers. Do you want to call an 800 number and get a different person every time you have a question? How comfortable are you with sharing your financial situation with a different stranger each time you call for assistance? Without help from one consistent person who knows your situation, it is difficult to navigate the complexities of personal finance. You may cost yourself thousands of dollars because of mistakes you would have avoided with an advisor's help.

For example, suppose you log into your online account to do a Roth conversion (we'll cover this in more detail in Chapter 14) and accidentally convert your entire $2 million IRA instead of $20,000? That mistake will cost you $740,000 in federal income taxes if you are in the 37 percent tax bracket! You might think, "No biggie. I'll just call and tell them my mistake so they can fix it." However, under current laws, there is no do-over for a Roth conversion like there used to be.

An advisor would have looked at your entire financial situation and determined whether a Roth conversion made sense before executing this transaction in the first place. If it made sense, the advisor would have chosen the correct amount to convert!

Why Evidence-Based Investing Works

Now that we know what *doesn't* work when it comes to investing our money, let's evaluate what *does* work. Knowing what works is critical to your investing success. Evidence-based investing eliminates market timing, picking individual stocks, and chasing manager performance by incorporating Nobel Prize–winning academic theories about how markets work.

The first theory is the *efficient market hypothesis*, which states that the markets are priced correctly. The price a stock is trading at today is a fair price, and no one can take advantage of mispricing. The next component is market factors. You want to own small companies as well as value companies.

Another theory incorporated into evidence-based investing is the *modern portfolio theory*. This theory is based on a diversified portfolio in which returns are maximized based on risk level. Finally, you want to understand behavior and avoid emotional investing decisions.

Efficient Market Hypothesis

If you can't beat the markets, what should you do? Join them! They are great wealth-creation tools. Figure 7 shows market returns by asset class compared to inflation.

What is a market return?

Asset	Return (1/1994 – 12/2020)
S&P 500	10.17%
5 Year US Government Treasury Bonds	4.82%
One-Month Treasury Bills	2.31%
Inflation	2.17%

*S&P 500 Index data from Standard and Poors Financial Services. Five Year US Gov't Treasury Bonds and One-month Treasury Bills Data from United States Treasury, Inflation data from United States Federal Reserve. This graph shows historical information and is for illustrative purposes only. Past performance does not guarantee future results.

Figure 7[6]

The goal of investing is to outpace inflation—something treasury bills barely did during the time period covered. Inflation erodes your wealth and spending power, because your money is worth less tomorrow than it is today. As the figure shows, the market did well. The more conservative investments come with less risk and smaller returns.

Most people think that it is impossible to accumulate a million dollars in their lifetime. That's not true. You can accumulate at least a million dollars in your lifetime if you save and invest appropriately. Don't speculate and gamble. Figure 8 shows how this is possible.

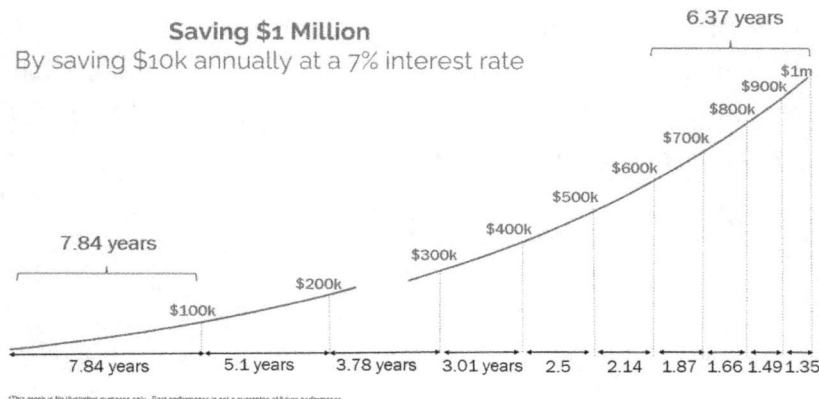

Figure 8[7]

© 2020 Evidence Based Advisors. Used by permission.

Suppose you invest $10,000 a year and earn 7 percent. The first $100,000 is the hardest to accumulate through compound interest; it takes 7.84 years. Einstein called compound interest the eighth wonder of the world, and he was right! You will accumulate the next $100,000 in only 5.1 years due to compound interest. The last $400,000 takes less time to accumulate than the first $100,000! Thank you, compound interest!

Market Factors and the Modern Portfolio Theory

Why should you include small companies in your portfolio? Because all large companies started out as small companies. Apple, Amazon, Facebook, and Google all started out in someone's garage or college dorm room. Small companies have higher expected returns and can greatly diversify a portfolio. Look at the evidence in Figure 9.

Figure 9[8]

Value companies are distressed for one reason or another. They become growth companies when they get healthier. This translates into higher expected returns. Some big-name companies were once distressed and have seen tremendous growth over the years. Apple almost went out of business in the 1990s; the same was true of Nintendo in the early 2000s, Delta in the mid-2000s, Starbucks in 2008, and Netflix in 2011. No one knows which company will turn things around from distress to growth—that's why you should own them all.

Figure 10 provides evidence to support why value companies should be added to your portfolio.

Figure 10[9]

Again, stay diversified and have small, value, and large companies in your portfolio. Diversification is your friend. You don't want to put all your eggs in one basket; in other words, don't invest all your money in one stock, sector, or country.

Avoiding Emotional Investing Decisions with the Help of a Financial Planner

You are most likely your worst enemy when it comes to investing, because it's your hard-earned money, and you are so attached to it. That's why it's so important to work with a trusted advisor who can help you navigate the cycle of emotions you will experience as an investor. Markets don't go up in a straight line. There are ups and downs along the way. It's like an emotional roller coaster.

When the market is going up, people get excited. They hear on the news about all-time market highs. That gets them excited, and they want in. So, they invest. Then, the market drops. And drops. And drops some more. People worry, panic, and sell at the bottom. Then the cycle starts again. Most investors buy high and sell low because of emotions. In reality, it's best to buy low and sell high.

Humans have 188 cognitive biases that have been around since the beginning of time. These biases will destroy your portfolio. Your perception of reality, based on your experiences, dictates your behavior. A trusted advisor takes the emotion out of investing and keeps you invested so you can reach your financial goals. Figure 11 shows the emotions an investor experiences.

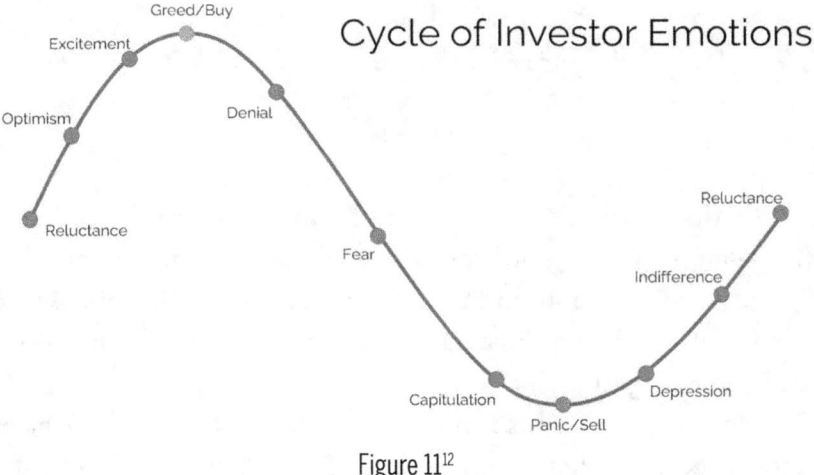

Figure 11[12]

© 2020 Evidence Based Advisors. Used by permission.

Figure 12 further proves the point that investors make emotional decisions.

Diversification and the Average Investor
2001-2020 (20 Years)

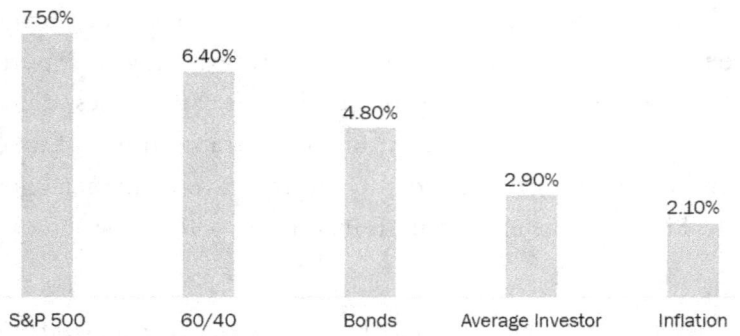

Source: Barclays, Bloomberg, FactSet, Standard & Poor's, J.P. Morgan Asset Management; (Bottom) Dalbar Inc. MSCI, NAREIT, Russell. Indices used are as follows: REITs: NAREIT Equity REIT Index; Small Cap: Russell 2000, EM Equity: MSCI EM, DM Equity: MSCI EAFE, Commodity: Bloomberg Commodity Index, High Yield: Bloomberg Barclays Global HY Index, Bonds: Bloomberg Barclays U.S. Aggregate Index; Homes: median sale price of existing single-family homes, Cash: Bloomberg Barclays 1-3m Treasury; Inflation: CPI. 60/40: A balanced portfolio with 60% invested in S&P 500 Index and 40% invested in high-quality U.S. fixed income, represented by the Bloomberg Barclays U.S. Aggregate Index. The portfolio is rebalanced annually. Average asset allocation investor return is based on an analysis by Dalbar Inc., which utilizes the net of aggregate mutual fund sales, redemptions and exchanges each month as a measure of investor behavior. Guide to the Markets – U.S. Data are as of June 30, 2021.

Figure 12[13]

As the figure shows, the average investor barely beats inflation—more evidence proving that working with an advisor adds 3 percent to your bottom line. Why not live your life doing what you do best, enjoying time with family and friends, and not worrying about figuring out how to invest?

Most people speculate and gamble. Most of those who *do* have knowledge about how to invest *don't* have a handle on the scary emotions that come up time and time again. As your account balances grow, fear starts to creep in, and you are likely to succumb to your emotions. Even the most sophisticated investors succumb to emotions at some point.

In March 2020, I had a client who claimed he had exclusive information about economic conditions and that the market was headed for a crash, so he wanted to move his portfolio to cash. He was sure things were going to get even worse. Fortunately, he didn't move to cash. The market recovered, and my clients were positive for the year. If he had moved to cash, he would have missed out on the recovery. No one knows precisely when to get in and when to get out of the market. Allow yourself the financial peace of mind that comes from relying on evidence and professional help instead of going it alone.

Moving to Cash Is the Worst Thing You Can Do to Your Portfolio

When markets are volatile, people get scared. When they turn on the news, they become even more afraid of investing. The worst thing you can do during volatile times is move your portfolio to cash. The one thing you can be certain of when you move to cash is that you have locked in your losses.

Humans don't like to suffer any losses, perceived or real. As we learned in Chapter 5, this is just another money block that needs to be cleared. If you suffer from this block, take a moment right now and follow the steps laid out in Chapter 5 to release the block before reading further.

During one period of volatility, a new client wanted me to manage his retirement savings, which he wasn't planning on using for another thirteen years. He had been managing it on his own but kept losing money. He would make gains, and then the market would go down, and he'd get scared and move to cash. The day after he signed on as a client, the market was down 600 points. He was sitting in cash but wanted me to wait before I invested his account because he thought the market would go down further.

However, accounts don't move immediately. The firm sending money and the firm receiving it both have to review all the paperwork. In addition, the market was up the very next day. It doesn't matter when you invest, because how long your money is in the market is more important than trying to time the market.

I explained to my client that he had been trying to time the market—that's how he had arrived at his current position. Now that he had hired me, he had a strategy. I determined his emotional risk score and built a low-cost portfolio around that number. We stayed invested in good and bad times, and we took advantage of the bad times by rebalancing.

Rebalancing is when you bring a portfolio back into alignment with its original design. You buy or sell a portion of each holding so that the percentage of the portfolio invested in each holding is in line with prior allocations. By doing so, you essentially buy low and sell high.

Nobody can time the market because nobody has a crystal ball. In 2015, CNBC gave an example of a really bad market timer.[19] An investor (let's call him Bob) began investing in 1973 over a 42-year time horizon. He put $6,000 into the S&P 500 before the market dropped 48 percent. He was upset, but he stayed invested. However, he didn't deposit any more money into his account until he felt comfortable again. He was brave enough to invest right before the 1987 crash, when he deposited $46,000 into his account—everything he had saved up to that point. After the 1987 crash, Bob was leery of investing again, and he didn't get back into the market until 2000, when he put $68,000 into his account—only to see the market crash in 2001. Bob had the worst luck! In 2007, he put in another $64,000, and we all know what happened in 2008. The market crashed yet again! But before you start feeling sorry for poor Bob, let's look at the amount of money he ended up with.

Over 42 years, he invested a total of $184,000. During that time, his investments grew to $1.6 million dollars! That is a total return of about 9 percent. His profit was over a million dollars.

You are probably scratching your head right now, wondering how Bob made so much money. After all, he had the worst luck, and every time he invested, the market crashed shortly thereafter.

His profit was the result of *staying invested* and not moving his portfolio to cash when he got scared. If history teaches us one thing, it is that the market always recovers. The best time to invest is today. No one knows when the market is going to be at its peak or when it will hit bottom except in retrospect.

Now, let's look at a 20-year time horizon of investing in the S&P 500 from 1999 to 2018 using information from a 2019 study by Capital Group/American Funds.[20] Suppose an investor put $10,000 in the market on the best day—that is, when the market was at its low point for the year—every year for those 20 years. In December 2018, at the end of 20 years, he would have had $546,793, a 9.16 percent average annual rate of return.

Suppose another investor also put in $10,000 a year over the same time horizon but put his money in on the worst days—when the market was at its peak each year. He would have had a 6.91 percent average annual rate of return and an ending balance of $415,460.

Both investors had positive returns because they didn't move to cash when the market became volatile during the tech bubble in 2001 and the housing crisis that led to the 2008 recession. Time in the market—not trying to time the market—is what is important. Just get in and hold on.

You might hear your friends at work saying, "Oh, I moved my money to cash, and then I put money in this fund, and my account is up 20 percent." That may be true, but the results are due to luck, and luck is not a long-term strategy. To get the same return as your friend, you both have to put your money into the market at the same time. If you put your money in after your friend already earned a 20 percent return, it's too late. You will not receive the same return. Following what a friend just did is not the way to invest for your future—that's why I stress the importance of working with a CFP® professional.

If you invest with me, the first thing I do is determine your risk tolerance. I also determine your emotional risk score, which tells me what you really feel. I need that information because we're going to talk about your actual numbers, and then we're going to build a portfolio to match that number.

When the markets are doing well, you think, "Life is great." But when there's market volatility, I am there to reassure you that your plan is on track and remind you that we prepared for the market's ups and downs. This is where I earn my keep. I'm not going to let you run to cash. I'm going to hold your hand through it all, giving you financial peace of mind, because I am there to help you reach your financial goals. I help by teaching you to leave emotions out of investing by partnering with so you don't have to go it alone any longer.

Vanguard did a study that showed that working with a financial advisor adds 3 percent to your bottom line.[21] You will more than make up for a financial advisor's fee, which is nominal compared to what you could lose by investing on your own. In fact, many do-it-yourself investors experience negative returns.

For the past 91 years, the S&P 500 has had ups and downs every year. About 27 years had negative results in a one-year time frame, meaning if you went out to cash in one year and didn't stay invested, you would have really lost 27 of those years. Now, if you stayed invested for just three years, you would have experienced half of those negative year periods. If you went out for 10 years, you would only experience five of those negative periods.

I cannot stress enough how important it is to stay in the market. It might seem like a risky thing to do, but all the evidence shows that if you stay in the market, you reap the rewards.

CHAPTER 13

One Of the Best Places to Save Your Money

Most people use a bank account as the place to save their money. They either keep it in checking, savings, or both. This wasn't a horrible idea when interest rates were higher, but these days, you are barely earning any interest in bank accounts. In today's world, the real purpose of bank accounts is not to grow your money, but to provide liquidity and use and control of money earned elsewhere.

What if I told you there is a way to store money and have it grow at a higher rate than what the bank offers? Would you want to know about that account? More importantly, would you actually use it? If you answered yes to the last two questions, you are in luck! Such an account does exist! Before I tell you what kind of account I'm describing, let me highlight its features and how it works.

This mystery account has the same features as a savings account—liquidity, use, and control of your money—plus much more. You can access your money at any time, use it for anything you want, and you own the account. However, not all the money you put in is available to you at the beginning of the contract. It takes a few years before the policy breaks even.

This account differs from a savings account in that it earns uninterrupted compound interest whether you use the money or not. You might be wondering, "How can my account still earn interest if I take the money out? If I take money out of my savings account, isn't that money gone?"

Actually, with this mystery account, you aren't taking *your* money out of the account. You are borrowing the financial institution's money and leaving your money in the account to earn interest through a process known as collateralization. The financial institution loans you the money. Typically, you have the option to *not* repay this kind of loan—another benefit of setting up this kind of account and borrowing in this manner. If you choose not to repay, the institution recovers what it is owed from your account, which serves as collateral to secure loan repayment. (However, I recommend that you be a good banker and repay what you owe with interest so you can continue to build wealth.)

Another way the institution can recover such a loan is by deducting it from the death benefit. When a loan is repaid in this way, you are essentially borrowing from your dead self. Suppose the death benefit is $500,000. You take out a loan for $50,000. If you die, your beneficiary receives $450,000 instead of $500,000, because $50,000 goes toward repaying the loan.

In retirement, you won't need to pay back loans from this type of account as long as they are structured properly. To ensure that they're structured properly, you need the advice of a good financial planner. If you allow the policy to lapse by taking out too much money, you may have a taxable event.

This kind of account also features tax-deferred growth and tax-free distribution. Tax-deferred growth means you do not pay taxes each year on the growth of your money. You won't receive a 1099 tax statement at the end of each year, as you do with a savings or investment account. Savings and investment accounts funded with pre-tax money are considered taxable accounts; that's why you get a 1099 statement for earnings on these accounts.

What is even better than tax-deferred? You guessed it: tax-free! When you take money out of this type of account, it is tax-free in the form of loans or withdrawals up to the amount of money that you have paid into the account (this amount is called the *basis*).

A typical savings account earns perhaps .001 percent. How would you like an account that has a competitive long-term rate of return? This type of account does. It earns dividends and uninterrupted compound interest. The interest rate on the dividends is 4 to 4.7 percent. Remember, these earnings are tax-free, and dividends are not guaranteed. However, I work with companies that have paid consistent dividends.

Another benefit of this type of account is that it allows for high contributions. Contributions are not limited like they are in a 401(k), Roth IRA, or traditional IRA. There are no income limitations as there are with a Roth IRA, making this type of account a great option for high-income earners who are ineligible to contribute to a Roth IRA. The account can be structured so that you can contribute as much as you want, subject to insurability and the insurance company's limit for your age and income.

The next feature of this type of account is a guaranteed loan option. This benefit was particularly useful during the pandemic. Some of my clients took out loans from their accounts while they were waiting for stimulus checks and/or PPP loans. To get a loan from this type of account, you simply call the company and ask for it. Within a couple of days, the money is in your bank account. You don't have to fill out a long application, show proof of income, or wait to find out if your loan was approved. And *you* get to decide when to repay the loan.

Those that didn't have this type of account during the pandemic may have had to wait for unemployment checks, which were often delayed. Others tried to take out home equity loans or lines of credit, but many banks (e.g., Wells Fargo) stopped issuing home equity loans during the pandemic.

If you lose your job and try to refinance or get a home equity loan, your application is likely to be denied, because banks want assurance that you can repay the loan. If that's the case, why are we in such a rush to pay off our homes. If you try to use your home to get money during an emergency, you may be in a bind. If all your money is tied up in your house, the only ways to get at that money are to sell the house or arrange for a new line of credit, which often come with fees and closing costs that could have been avoided if you didn't rush to pay off your home. We are in a seller's market as I write this. You will get a great price for your house, but where are you going to live? The other houses on the market will also have higher price tags.

If you can't get your money from your house, where else can you get it? Some people have money in the stock market. But if all your money is in the stock market, you don't want to take it out. When the market is doing well, you don't want to miss out on gains, and when the market is down, you don't want to lock in your losses.

The pandemic year of 2020 was certainly one of clear vision. What you have been led to believe about money by many so-called experts isn't the whole truth. Paying off your house and putting all your money in the market isn't a complete financial plan. The pandemic highlighted access to capital as a critical but often overlooked feature of a financial plan. Fortunately for you, this book gives you the strategies you need to build your wealth.

Like money in a savings account, the money in this mystery account is safe. In fact, the guaranteed cash value of the account is not limited, unlike the FDIC limit of $250,000 on your checking or savings account. The money you contribute and the interest you earn are guaranteed and not subject to market volatility or losses. The only way you lose money with this type of account is if you cancel the account prematurely or if a loan balance lapses the policy. Remember, this is a long-term strategy. Discipline is key when it comes to saving continuously. Money in this account is also liquid.

How great would it be to have a loan that you pay back on your terms—potentially not even during your lifetime? That is one of the greatest features of this account. Being able to determine your own repayment schedule provides you with great flexibility. As mentioned previously, your loan doesn't have to be paid back, but I strongly urge you to do so during your accumulation years. (However, as covered in Chapter 10, pay off higher interest rate debts before paying off loans secured by this type of account.) Aim to repay what you withdrew with interest, because that's how you build wealth. However, do so with a smart plan in mind.

Some additional benefits of this type of account are creditor protection, depending on the state you live in, and disability protection. If you cannot make contributions to this account and you have disability protection, the institution will pay the contributions for you. You can't get that from a savings account! When you die, the account pays a death benefit. The death benefit is always *at least* the value of the cash account and almost always more. The death benefit is also tax-free.

All these benefits sound great, but what is this mystery account we are talking about? It's permanent cash-value life insurance. The foregoing benefits are specific to whole life insurance.

Now, before you bail on reading the rest of this book, please take a deep breath and set aside everything you have heard about life insurance. The IRS tax code has changed in many ways, and the product I am introducing is relatively new. So, I suggest going back to the chapter on releasing money blocks and walking through the exercise if this is a block for you.

For permanent cash-value life insurance to work in the way I have described, it has to be structured so as to maximize the cash value and minimize the death benefit. The IRS has set rules on exactly how much can be contributed to this type of account without it becoming taxable, so it is important to work with a licensed agent—preferably someone who also has the CFP® designation—when setting it up.

Essentially, you pay more premium than is required to maintain the death benefit for the policy. This is known as overfunding a policy. Many agents aren't aware that you can do this with life insurance, so you need to find an agent who knows how to design a policy for your benefit. Agents are paid a commission based on death benefits: The higher the death benefit, the higher their commission. So, they might want to sell you a policy with the highest possible death benefit. Although it means being paid less, I want to do the opposite, because I want to help you.

If you are using a whole life policy, you can choose how long you want to pay premiums. Some policies are paid up after 10 or 20 years; others are paid up at age 65. There are even some where you can pay until you are 100 years old and still receive tax-deferred growth and tax-free withdrawals! Even if you have a policy that can be paid to 100 years old, you don't have to pay the premiums, because at some point, the dividends will be large enough to pay the premiums for you. Clients who want to continue tax-deferred growth can choose to continue making payments. There are other options if you don't want to pay the premium, but when you see the cash value increasing by more than the premium payment, you may not want to stop paying the premium. You have options on what you want to do with the policy.

Who Shouldn't Have an Overfunded Life Insurance Policy?

Although this type of policy is a great addition to your financial plan, an overfunded life insurance policy is not for everyone. Let's explore why an overfunded policy might *not* work for you and some alternatives.

Age and Health

The cost of insurance increases with age. The younger and healthier you are, the lower the cost of the insurance will be. If you don't have a good health rating, this strategy isn't the best way for you to save. If all you need is a death benefit, an overfunded permanent cash-value policy like this is too costly and is an inefficient use of your money. A different policy design would better suit your needs.

Not Enough Saved

In order to reap the benefits, you should plan on paying between $5,000 and $10,000 into this policy annually. Ideally, aim for $10,000, because the more you put into the policy, the more it grows. If you don't have that amount to contribute each year, you may want to get a term life insurance policy from a reputable company—not necessarily the cheapest policy you can find. Make sure the policy is convertible to a strong whole life or indexed universal life policy in the future. That way, you lock in your health rating and insurability, and you will not have to go through underwriting when you are able to afford the permanent policy.

You Want to See Immediate Results

This is a long-term strategy, as in 10 to 20 years or longer. That kind of time horizon is when you will see the power of compounding and cash value. Discipline is key. If you are not used to saving on a monthly, quarterly, or annual basis or are not willing to commit to a long-term savings strategy, this is not a strategy for you. You will probably see cash value in the first year of the policy, but it won't be equal to what you paid in premiums. Remember, it's life insurance. In traditionally funded policies where you only pay the premium required to support the death benefit, you don't see cash value until the third year. The break-even point on overfunded policies is usually about seven to 10 years. From then on, the cash value is more than the premiums you have paid. The longer you own the policy, the more it compounds exponentially. It's the time value of money and the uninterrupted compounding effect. When you reach the point where you use your policy for retirement income, you will most likely pull out more income than you have paid into the policy in premiums according to the whole life illustrations I've run. However, you don't have to wait to start borrowing money against your policy. You can borrow money as soon as there is cash value. If you aren't concerned with accessing the cash value, again, this might not be right for you.

Who Should Have an Overfunded Policy?

This strategy works for someone who is looking to maximize cash flow by using a policy like this to finance major capital purchases, such as cars and business equipment. It's also a key component of a financial plan for someone who is looking to maximize retirement cash flow, minimize taxes in retirement, and have a plan for market volatility. We'll cover how to make major capital purchases and how retirement plans work in Chapter 14.

Other Policy Options

If you are strictly looking for tax-free retirement income, you need a policy design that provides a larger income stream in retirement. I like whole life insurance because of the guarantees it provides, and the companies that I write pay dividends. If you want the potential to have higher cash value, then you should consider indexed universal life (IUL) insurance policies.

Here's how an IUL policy works. If you are using an IUL policy, there are no dividends. It earns interest based on the index you select (i.e., the S&P 500 index). Each company has its own indexing strategy. Some strategies are capped, while other strategies are uncapped. Here's an example. Suppose your cash value is in the S&P 500 index, and it earns 15 percent. If your contract states that the policy is capped at 10 percent, then 10 percent is credited to your cash-value account. If the index earns 4 percent, then 4 percent is credited to your cash-value account. If the policy is uncapped, you receive whatever percentage the index earns. I won't get into the nitty-gritty here. I just want to make you aware of another permanent life policy you can overfund.

If you are looking for protection and a lot of coverage, term insurance or a blend of term insurance and permanent insurance may be right for you. If you are looking for a low-cost permanent death benefit to transfer wealth to the next generation, then a guaranteed universal life or low-cost universal life policy may be right for you.

Given all the options, it's definitely worthwhile to work with a financial professional who is willing to take the time to get to know you and your individual situation and who is familiar with how to structure insurance properly for your needs. Not all whole life policies or IUL's are created the same, each life insurance carrier has different features. It is best to have a professional help you choose the carrier and type of insurance that is best for you. If you have someone, great! If not, you can reach out to me, and I'd be happy to help.

Go to my website at:

www.dsfinancialstrategies.com

and schedule a complimentary consultation.

CHAPTER 14

How to Use Your Overfunded Life Insurance Policy as Your Bank

First, I want to make it clear that an overfunded life insurance policy is something to include in your financial plan *in addition* to your banking accounts. You cannot replace the bank entirely. However, a properly designed life insurance policy is a great place for long-term savings.

Contrary to popular belief, you finance everything you buy. Even if you pay cash, you are giving up the interest you could have earned on your money. Banks don't lose interest, and neither should you.

Let's look at how banks work. To be profitable, banks need our money. We walk into a bank, give them our hard-earned money, and these days, they pay us .001 percent interest. Once the bank has our money, they can lend out nine times the amount we deposit. This practice is called fractional reserve banking.

Fractional reserve banking boils down to this: You find a bank that will give you 2 percent interest on your money. They use your money to write a personal loan at 10 percent, a car loan at 4 percent, a fifteen-year mortgage at 2.5 percent, and so on. Banks are one of the most profitable businesses in the world, which is why you see one on almost every corner. They tell us to leave our money with them for as long as possible, but they don't follow that advice—they lend it out as soon as possible!

When you structure an overfunded life insurance policy correctly, you are creating your own bank. You put your money in the policy through premiums, which are equivalent to deposits in your bank account. Your policy should be structured so that most of the premium goes to the paid-up additions (PUA) rider, a savings component that allows you to pay more premiums than are required to keep the policy enforced. The policy should also be structured with the *minimum* death benefit for the value of the premiums you are paying into the policy, thereby lowering the cost of insurance.

The policy earns interest and dividends. Your money earns *uninterrupted* compound interest, because when you withdraw money from the policy via a loan, you aren't borrowing *your* money—you are borrowing the *insurance company's* money. That means your money continues to grow, uninterrupted.

Make sure you work with an insurance company that offers non-direct recognition. Non-direct recognition means the insurance company does not reduce the amount of your account on which you are paid a dividend when there is a loan against the policy. Instead, they treat the loan separately and continue to pay a dividend on the account value without any deduction for the loan amount. In other words, they don't "recognize" that you took out a loan.

Those are the basics of how to set up a life insurance policy to function as your "bank." There's a lot more detail to it—that's why working with a good financial planner or insurance agent who knows the ins and outs of policy design is so important.

Once you have set up your insurance policy "bank," how do you use it? Many people use this strategy to purchase cars, pay for weddings, pay for college, and so forth.

For example, here's how it works if you want to buy a car. First, you have to pay the premiums until there is sufficient cash value for you to take out a loan to cover the cost of the car. Remember, this is a long-term strategy, so you won't see immediate results. You won't be able to buy a car immediately after opening the account; you might be able to use this strategy to buy a car after five years.

Suppose you are paying $12,000 a year in premiums. After five years, you have roughly $51,000 in cash value. You want to buy a car that costs $25,000, so you take out a $25,000 loan against the policy. Then, to pay the loan back, you make payments of $5,000 to $6,000 a year for the next five years, plus interest (which you don't mind paying, because you are paying it to yourself in your own "bank"). You also continue paying the premiums, so you spend $17,000 to $18,000 out of pocket for those five years. Rather than paying a bank $6,000 a year, you are putting $6,000 a year into *your* "bank."

You can do this every time you purchase a car. If you miss a payment on a traditional car loan, they may repossess your car. However, you can skip a payment on a loan from the insurance company if you need to. Again, I caution against this, because you want to be a good banker. But if there's an emergency, you have that flexibility. Another benefit of purchasing a car this way is that, although you have a loan against the policy, your cash value is still earning uninterrupted compound interest.

Remember, this strategy only works for people who are savers, because you still have to pay the premiums. Think of the premiums as what you would deposit into a savings account each year.

Here's a personal story of what can happen if you are undisciplined in paying your life insurance policy. I took out a loan for almost the maximum allowed by my policy, and I never paid it back. It was for something stupid, too. I planned to open a new policy and pay double the premium I had been paying for the first policy. But you can't make up lost time accruing interest. We are all human, and sometimes make poor choices. My choices in this case were things I would *never* advise my clients to do. I ended up canceling the new policy, too. The problem was that I didn't have the discipline to repay the loan on my policy.

What happened next highlights the fact that I should have stuck with my original life insurance policy and repaid the loan. I wanted to finish paying off a car loan, so I attempted to do a cash-out refinance on my rental property. My rental property would still have been profitable—even with the cash-out—and I would have freed up $550 a month in extra cash flow. The problem was, after I provided the bank with a ton of documentation, they turned down my loan.

All my money was trapped in my house, and there was nothing I could do about it. If I had kept my first insurance policy in place and repaid the loan I took out on it, I could have just called the insurance company when I wanted to pay off my car loan and received the money within 24 hours—a far easier way to free up $550 a month in cash flow. Yes, I would have had to repay the policy loan back, but it would have been on my terms. I would have been able to decide how much to repay and when I wanted to pay it. Having an overfunded life insurance policy gives you liquidity, use, control, and freedom with your money.

How to Pay for College Without Going Broke

Paying for college is one of life's largest expenses. A four-year degree can cost as much as $250,000. Parents with multiple children often worry constantly about this expense. The good news is that, through proper planning, you can pay for college without going broke.

There are many types of accounts that allow you to save money for educational purposes in a tax-favored manner.

The 529 plan is one of the most popular of these types of accounts. If a 529 plan is used specifically for college, the money in the account is nontaxable, and it also grows tax-free within the account. While those are both wonderful benefits, there are several drawbacks to using a 529 plan for college expenses.

A 529 plan is usually invested in mutual funds, so it is subject to market fluctuations. This can be positive or negative. For example, if you lose money in a bad market and it comes time to pay for college, you may not have as much money as you would if you were making withdrawals in an up market.

A colleague of mine experienced a different type of drawback to a 529 plan. His son received a full scholarship, but they had to spend everything in the 529 plan before he could receive any scholarship funds.

If the money in a 529 plan is not used for college, the earnings in the account will be taxed at your current bracket, and the IRS may impose a 10 percent penalty. The law recently changed. As of 2023, if you have had an account for 15 years or longer, you can roll it over into a Roth IRA. Clearly, there are pros and cons to setting up a 529 plan. Consider these factors and plan carefully before jumping in!

Another option for paying for college—in my opinion, one of the most underutilized and misunderstood asset classes—is cash-value life insurance. Modern cash-value life insurance policies have many new and innovative living benefits in addition to providing a tax-efficient strategy for accumulating money that can be used to fund a child's college education or your retirement.

The cash value grows tax-deferred. If the policy is structured and utilized properly, the cash can be taken out from the policy tax-free. Life insurance is also one of the few assets not counted on the Free Application for Federal Student Aid (FAFSA) form. Thus, if you fund a life insurance policy instead of a bank account, you appear to have fewer assets available to pay for college, and your child may receive more federal student aid.

When choosing a college, don't automatically assume that state schools are cheaper. In many cases, a private school costs less than a state school given the same level of student financial need. This is because private schools usually have larger endowments and fewer students, which allows them to offer more aid regardless of the parents' income and assets.

The sooner you start planning and saving for your child, the better. If your child is already in high school, it's not too late to save. You can design a life insurance policy to lower your effective family contribution (EFC)—the amount a college requires you to pay if your child attends that school.

Reasons You Should Have a Mortgage

There are four reasons to have a mortgage:
1. You don't have enough cash to pay for your house.
2. You can claim a tax deduction for mortgage interest.
3. Money in your pocket may be able to earn more than it costs to borrow money.
4. Most important: A mortgage enables you to have liquidity, use, and control of your money.

If you don't have enough money to pay cash for a house, it's obvious you need to have a mortgage.

Now, let's consider inflation. The most valuable dollars you have are the ones you have in your pocket today. In today's dollars, a $2,000 monthly mortgage payment with 3 percent inflation will feel like $823.97 in 30 years. Your money will never be worth more than it is today. Wouldn't you rather hold on to your most valuable dollars?

What if you have enough money to pay cash for a $300,000 house? If you keep your money instead of buying the house and earn 6 percent on your $300,000 for 30 years, you will have $1,806,773. If you pay cash for the house—here is your opportunity cost, your loss of potential gain—your money is now invested in your house and earning zero percent. I'll come back to that in a minute.

If you take out a 30-year mortgage at 4.5 percent, your monthly payment will be $1,520. The total cost to own your $300,000 home (principal, interest, and opportunity) is $1,526,919. It makes sense to have a mortgage, because your money can earn more than the mortgage is costing you.

Now, let's factor in the tax deduction. If you are in the 30 percent tax bracket, the net cost to borrow is 3.15 percent, and the total cost to have the mortgage is $1,295,031. Not everyone can claim the mortgage deduction, so be sure to check with your tax adviser. With a 30-year mortgage, you can claim a higher deduction in the first 15 years than you can if you have a 15-year mortgage. As you can see, the potential spread and tax deduction make it a wise decision to have a mortgage.

Of course, there are advantages to renting, too (e.g., you don't have to pay property taxes), so always look at the pros and cons when making housing decisions.

Finally, let's talk about control. As I mentioned previously, the money (equity) in your house earns zero percent. Equity is not determined by how much money you have in the house but by appreciation, which is the increase in the property's value over time. Why would you want to tie up your money in something that earns zero percent? The only way to access this money is to borrow against or sell your house. What if you lose your job, become disabled, or your home is destroyed by a natural disaster? If your money is in your house, you will be unable to access the equity. If your money is in an account that you can readily access, you can weather the storm until your circumstances change. At some point, your side fund will be enough to pay off your house if you choose to do so.

Knowing what you know now, do you want to give up your most valuable dollars? I don't.

In Case of a Natural Disaster, Should You or Your Bank Own Your House?

What comes to mind when you think of protecting your house from natural disasters, such as hurricanes or floods? Most people rely on homeowner's or flood insurance to keep them comfortable; that's what we pay for. If your house is destroyed by a natural disaster, your insurance company will pay to have it repaired, and they will provide living assistance while progress is made. But everyone else in your community who lost their house will be in the same boat, and that can make finding a nearby, available hotel room within the budget or per diem of your insurance benefit very difficult. The living assistance you will receive is likely to translate into a standard room at a budget hotel.

In theory, this cushion is a comfort. But if there is a sudden, overwhelming demand for contractors, repairs are likely to take months, deflating your initial appreciation and confidence in your preparedness. It will be a while before you are back to living in your house and cooking your own meals. Unless you can afford to rent a home or walk away from the shell of your home, home and flood insurance coverage simply doesn't measure up.

Facing discomfort like this as a family in the wake of a disaster can lead to emotional financial decisions, which can be detrimental (as we learned in previous chapters). For example, some people may choose to tap into retirement accounts to boost their quality of life and cover basics not provided for by insurance, trying to recapture a sense of peace. Protecting your home's true value demands more than homeowner's insurance.

Most people feel more secure when their house is paid off. I believe you are more secure with a mortgage *and* a cash-value life insurance policy. This setup gives you access, liquidity, and control of your money when you need it. Let's look at three emotional and financial scenarios in which a mortgage and life insurance combination is beneficial.

In Scenario 1, you lose your job. So, you go to the bank to access some of your equity in the house. Your house is worth $500,000, and you owe $100,000 on your mortgage, which means you have access to $400,000. Not so fast! Because you don't have a job, the bank is worried about how you will repay them, and they won't give you a loan. All your money is tied up in your house. If your money was in a life insurance policy, you wouldn't need permission to access it.

In Scenario 2, you become disabled. Even if you have disability insurance and you have a big mortgage, as long as you have access to capital inside of a cash-value life insurance policy, you are in a better financial position than having no mortgage and no access to capital. This enables you to deal with your new circumstances.

In Scenario 3, your house is destroyed. If you have access to money in a cash-value life insurance policy, you can take out a loan, leave the motel, and rent an apartment until your house is rebuilt. The bank will be happy to give you a loan because you can use your life insurance as collateral. You also have the option to walk away from the house and deal with a bad credit score for seven years; that's not something I generally recommend, but in certain circumstances, it may be a good option. Properly funded life insurance is a protection strategy that homeowners ought to use.

You can pay off your house, but it is difficult to get a loan on your house when you really need it. The number one reason people want to have their house paid off is to eliminate the monthly payment. When you have your money in a safe place like a life insurance policy rather than in your house, eliminating the monthly payment can be accomplished without sacrificing protection. Do you want to own your house if it is destroyed in a natural disaster, or do you want the bank to?

The Truth About Qualified Retirement Plans

Retirement plans, for example, a qualified plan like your 401(k), do two things:

1. They *defer* the payment of taxes—which does not necessarily *save* money on taxes.
2. They defer the tax calculation.

Let me illustrate how qualified plans actually work. Suppose you arrange to borrow $10,000 from me. Before you take the money, you ask me when you have to pay it back and how much interest I will charge. I tell you that I don't need the money now, but at some time in the future when I need it, I will calculate how much interest you will have to pay me. Will you take the loan? No way! However, that is exactly what the government does with qualified plans.

There is value in putting money in a 401(k) up to the match—but not a penny more. Most people think that by retirement age, they will be in a lower tax bracket. Do you really want to reduce your standard of living, or do you just want to pay the least amount of taxes? You probably want to pay the least amount of taxes when you retire, but this isn't always the case. If you are in a lower tax bracket, you are better served by deferring taxes. Many financial planners—including me—believe that either tax rates will increase or the decision makers in Congress will lower the tax thresholds, resulting in the government being able to collect more money. Consequently, I do not believe you can realistically expect to be in a lower tax bracket.

The national debt is $31 trillion and rising, and we haven't even seen the biggest wave of baby boomers retiring yet. Seventy percent of baby boomers will retire between 2022 and 2030. Most Americans have their wealth in their retirement plans. To increase tax revenue, the government is likely to go after those who have money—baby boomer retirees. Therefore, the odds that you will be in a lower tax bracket are very low.

Most people commute to work every day in cars that are usually financed and typically replaced every three to five years. They overfund retirement plans at work so they can take a tax deduction, and they hurry to pay off their homes so they can really start saving for retirement. In doing this, they received a deduction through their 401(k) plan only to lose a deduction in their home mortgage. Qualified plans have many inefficiencies.

Whose retirement dream are you chasing—yours or Uncle Sam's?

Let's look at what happens when you're ready to use the money in your 401(k) for retirement. The numbers are rounded for ease of understanding.

Suppose every year for 35 years, you put $6,000 into your 401(k), a total contribution of $210,000. We will assume you are in the 32 percent tax bracket. On the surface, your tax savings are $2,000 a year—$6,000 × 32 percent. After 35 years, you have $70,000 in "tax savings." Assuming you have earned 7.5 percent interest over the 35 years, your account balance is $1,000,000. You are afraid to spend the principal, because you don't want to run out of money. So, you only withdraw the interest.

Figure 13 illustrates this example.

	$ 1,000,000	
X	7.50%	
	$75,000	Retirement Income
X	32%	Tax Rate
	$ 24,000	Annual Tax
	$ 51,000	Net Spendable Income
	$ 70,000	Tax Savings for 35yrs
	$ 72,000	Taxes in 1st 3 Retirement Years
	$ 480,000	Total tax by year 20

Figure 13

In this example, you "saved" $70,000 in taxes only to end up paying $480,000 in taxes over a 20-year retirement. By the third year, you have already paid more in taxes than you saved over 35 years—and that's if tax rates stay the same. I don't think they will.

The good news is that you have choices.

There are alternative ways to save money aside from qualified plans, including vehicles that let you enjoy a tax-free treatment.

As of 2023, if you are under the income limit for contributing to a Roth IRA, you can make the maximum allowable contribution to that account. (If your modified adjusted gross income is under $228,000 for married couples or under $153,000 for a single person, you can contribute to a Roth IRA.) As of 2023, if you are 50 years old or above, you can contribute up to $7,500 annually. For those people above the Roth IRA income limits, find out if your 401(k) has a Roth option. You might be able to direct a portion of your contribution to that.

Another option is a Roth conversion. A market downturn is an ideal time for a Roth conversion. A financial professional can help you evaluate whether a Roth conversion makes sense for you based on your particular financial situation. If you do a Roth conversion, make sure you have another source of funds to pay the resulting taxes so you don't have to take it from the IRA that you are converting. If you are receiving Social Security or on Medicare, find out if a Roth conversion will cause your Social Security payments to be taxed at a higher rate or cause your Medicare premiums to increase.

A Roth conversion is when you move money from a tax-deductible traditional IRA to a nondeductible Roth IRA. You pay tax on the funds when you move them to the Roth IRA, but once you hold the Roth IRA for five years, you don't pay taxes when you withdraw the funds or the gains from the funds in retirement. If money is withdrawn from a Roth IRA before retirement—depending on the reason for withdrawal—a portion of the withdrawal may be taxable. You can always get your contributions back tax-free. There are many rules regarding how and when you can withdraw money from a Roth IRA, so please check with your financial planner before doing so.

I don't want you to get the impression that your retirement plan is bad or that you shouldn't contribute to it. I just want to present a fuller picture regarding how to save for retirement. There is one other vehicle that is wise to include in a retirement plan; we will cover it in Chapter 15.

Using Life Insurance to Supplement Your Retirement

Life insurance is a great way to supplement your retirement income. I believe you should have two buckets of money in retirement: a risk bucket and a safe money bucket.

Let's talk about the safe bucket. Whole life insurance and IUL (also known as permanent life insurance) is similar to a Roth IRA—both vehicles allow for after-tax contributions, tax-deferred growth, and tax-free distribution. However, permanent life insurance has additional advantages: It doesn't have income or contribution limits. By now, you are familiar with the benefits of whole life insurance from the description in Chapter 13.

I already covered the contribution limits of a Roth IRA. Beyond the $6,500 (or $7,500 if you are 50+) a year Roth IRA contribution limit, the only other savings option with tax-free benefits is an overfunded life insurance, whole life, or indexed universal life policy. Life insurance policies can be structured to accept higher contributions, which can help if you are trying to catch up and build savings before you retire. Such policies are part of your safe bucket, because whole life insurance has guaranteed cash values and is not subject to market volatility like a Roth IRA is if it is invested in the market. You also have penalty-free access to your cash value before retirement, if necessary. Roth IRAs have restrictions on when and how you can get your money out.

Another way to use life insurance in your retirement plan is as a volatility buffer. Any money invested in the market is in your risk bucket. You need to have both buckets to use life insurance as a volatility buffer. When you are retired, you won't want to take money out of your retirement account when the market is down, because that will deplete your account sooner. If you have life insurance as part of your retirement plan, you can take the money out of your life insurance policy rather than your retirement account in down-market years.

To illustrate, let's look at a hypothetical example provided by Ohio National Financial Services.[1] Katherine is a 45-year-old attorney, and when she retires at 65, she will have $1.5 million in her retirement account. Her plan is to withdraw $100,000 a year for income. Conservatively, we project a 5 percent average annual return. After 10 years, Katherine still has more than $1.12 million. Figure 14 illustrates this example.

Katherine's Age	Account Balance on Jan. 1	Withdrawal on Jan. 1	Balance After Withdrawal	Average Annual Return	End of Year Account Balance	
65	$1,500,000	$100,000	$1,400,000	5.00%	$1,470,000	Note the consistent 5% average annual return each year.
66	$1,470,000	$100,000	$1,370,000	5.00%	$1,438,500	
67	$1,438,500	$100,000	$1,338,500	5.00%	$1,405,425	
68	$1,405,425	$100,000	$1,305,425	5.00%	$1,370,696	
69	$1,370,696	$100,000	$1,270,696	5.00%	$1,334,231	
70	$1,334,231	$100,000	$1,234,231	5.00%	$1,295,942	
71	$1,295,942	$100,000	$1,195,942	5.00%	$1,255,739	More than $1.12 million still available after 10 years of withdrawals.
72	$1,255,739	$100,000	$1,155,739	5.00%	$1,213,526	
73	$1,213,526	$100,000	$1,113,526	5.00%	$1,169,202	
74	$1,169,202	$100,000	$1,069,202	5.00%	$1,122,662	
				5.00% Annual Average Return		

Figure 14[2]

Note: Ohio National Financial Services. Life Insurance Retirement Supplement: Manage your retirement income with life insurance, 2020, p. 3.

This is unrealistic, because markets don't return 5 percent every year. In the real world, stock market returns are different every year.

Let's look at the actual returns for the S&P 500 between 2002 and 2011 and include them in Katherine's example. This is illustrated in Figure 15.

Katherine's Age	Year	Account Balance on Jan. 1	Withdrawal on Jan. 1	Balance After Withdrawal	S&P 500° Returns	End of Year Account Balance	
65	2002	$1,500,000	$100,000	$1,400,000	-22.10%	$1,090,600	The S&P 500™ is a commonly used indicator of overall U.S. stock market performance.
66	2003	$1,090,600	$100,000	$990,600	28.68%	$1,274,704	
67	2004	$1,274,704	$100,000	$1,174,704	10.88%	$1,302,512	
68	2005	$1,302,512	$100,000	$1,202,513	4.91%	$1,261,556	
69	2006	$1,261,556	$100,000	$1,161,556	15.79%	$1,344,966	More than $354,000 less than previous example. Katherine may not be able to withdraw $100,000 again due to her low account value.
70	2007	$1,344,966	$100,000	$1,244,966	5.49%	$1,313,315	
71	2008	$1,313,315	$100,000	$1,213,315	-37.00%	$764,388	
72	2009	$764,388	$100,000	$664,388	26.46%	$840,185	
73	2010	$840,185	$100,000	$740,185	15.10%	$851,953	
74	2011	$851,953	$100,000	$751,953	2.10%	$767,744	
					5.03% Annual Average Return		

Figure 15[3]

Note: Ohio National Financial Services. *Life Insurance Retirement Supplement: Manage your retirement income with life insurance*, 2020, p. 4.

Although the average annual rate is close to 5 percent, there is a difference of more than $354,000 in Katherine's final account balance. If she wants her income to last for the rest of her life, she needs to carefully decide if she should draw another $100,000 at the end of 10 years.

What if there was a way she could adjust her income withdrawals and manage negative market returns? She can if she doesn't take a withdrawal from her retirement account in the year following a market downturn.

Figure 16 shows that her account could be $319,795 higher than in the prior example at the end of 10 years if she doesn't take $100,000 withdrawals in any years following a market downturn.

No withdrawals the year
after a negative market.

Katherine's Age	Year	Account Balance on Jan. 1	Withdrawal on Jan. 1	Balance After Withdrawal	S&P 500 Returns	End of Year Account Balance
65	2002	$1,500,000	$100,000	$1,400,000	-22.10%	$1,090,600
66	2003	$1,090,600	$0	$1,090,600	28.68%	$1,403,384
67	2004	$1,403,384	$100,000	$1,303,384	10.88%	$1,445,192
68	2005	$1,445,192	$100,000	$1,345,192	4.91%	$1,411,241
69	2006	$1,411,241	$100,000	$1,311,241	15.79%	$1,518,286
70	2007	$1,518,286	$100,000	$1,418,286	5.49%	$1,496,150
71	2008	$1,496,150	$100,000	$1,396,150	-37.00%	$879,575
72	2009	$879,575	$0	$879,575	26.46%	$1,112,311
73	2010	$1,112,311	$100,000	$1,012,311	15.10%	$1,165,170
74	2011	$1,165,170	$100,000	$1,065,170	2.10%	$1,087,539

About **$319,795 more** than the previous example.

Figure 16[4]

Note: Ohio National Financial Services. *Life Insurance Retirement Supplement: Manage your retirement income with life insurance,* 2020, p. 5.

You are probably thinking, "That makes sense, but where is she going to get the income she needs to live on in those years?" That's where life insurance comes in. Instead of taking $100,000 out of her retirement account in the two years following down markets, she takes the money out of her insurance policy.

Figure 17 shows a whole life policy example. She receives the best health rating class and pays out-of-pocket premiums of $19,692 until age 65. Policy values (i.e., dividends and cash value) cover her premiums from ages 66 to 100.

End of Year Age	Policy Premium	Policy Loan Amount	Cash Value Increase (Current)*	Total Cash Surrender Value (Current)*	Total Death Benefit (Current)*
46	**$19,692**	–	$0	$0	$1,118,308
47	$19,692	–	$948	$948	$1,164,281
48	$19,692	–	$14,581	$15,529	$1,149,576
65	$19,692	–	$46,067	**$517,999**	$1,188,483
66	$19,692	–	$27,779	$545,778	$1,186,758
67	$19,692	$100,000	-$76,194	$469,583	$1,180,968
72	$19,692	–	$30,641	$608,074	$1,167,017
73	$19,692	$100,000	-$72,413	$535,661	$1,163,330
74	$19,692	–	$28,952	$564,613	$1,160,787
75	$19,692	–	$30,310	$594,923	**$1,159,392**

Annual premium of $19,692.

Income tax-free policy loans at ages 66 and 72 to balance negative returns on retirement savings.

Policy values cover premiums from age 66 to 100.

Current cash value grows to over $510,000 at age 65

A current death benefit of over $1.1 million at age 75.

* Using current dividend scale. Values shown use end-of-year ages and projected based on the current dividend scale and not guaranteed. For guaranteed values and other important information, see the sample illustration at the back of this brochure.

Note: The example assumes a $100,000 loan. However, because loans from certain life insurance policies are currently income tax-free under certain conditions, she would be able to take less money and still have the same after-tax cash flow as if she had taken the money from her retirement accounts.

Figure 17[5]

Note: Ohio National Financial Services. *Life Insurance Retirement Supplement: Manage your retirement income with life insurance*, 2020, p. 7.

It's a very smart move to life insurance as part of your retirement plan, not only as a volatility buffer but also for the long-term care benefits and the tax-free death benefit. If you need long-term care, you can access a portion of the death benefit to cover the cost. Some people hesitate to spend their money, because they want to leave money to their kids or grandkids. Having a life insurance gives you a "permission slip" to spend money.

CHAPTER 15

Protection Against Market Volatility

few years ago, ING bank ran a commercial asking, "What's your number?" The actors walked around with dollar amounts over their heads—the amount they needed to accumulate by the time they reached retirement age in order to retire the way they wanted to. I agree that it's good to know the amount of money you need in retirement. But the commercial didn't explain that it's possible to have the right number in your account and still run out of money during retirement—because of *sequence of returns risk*, which we will cover shortly. The point is that the decumulation phase is more important than the accumulation phase of retirement. You only get one shot to get it right. There are no do-overs if you run out of money. The question in retirement changes from "How much money do I have accumulated?" to "Do I have enough income to pay my bills this month?"

Sequence of returns risk is only a factor during the decumulation phase of retirement. Put simply, if you pull money out of your retirement account in a year when the market has negative returns, you will run out of money more quickly than if you withdraw when the market has positive returns. You can't change the year you were born, so you hope that in the year you retire (and the next couple of years after) the market is up.

Figure 18 shows two hypothetical couples who retire at age 65 with $1 million dollars. They plan to withdraw 6.5 percent ($65,000) a year for their retirement income. The illustration uses the S&P 500 index starting in 2000. For Mr. & Mrs. Jones, I use the S&P 500 returns in chronological order; for Mr. & Mrs. Smith, I use the S&P 500 returns in *reverse* chronological order.

SEQUENCE OF RETURNS RISK
Distribution Phase: $1,000,000

		Mr. & Mrs. Jones			Mr. & Mrs. Smith			Explanation
Year	Age	Annual Return	Portfolio Year-End Value	Withdrawals	Annual Return[1]	Portfolio Year-End Value[2]	Withdrawals	
2000	65	19.42%	$1,129,200	$ (65,000)	-10.14%	$833,600	$ (65,000)	1.) S&P 500 returns with no dividend reinvestment from 2017 - 2000 in
2001	66	9.54%	$1,171,926	$ (65,000)	-13.04%	$659,899	$ (65,000)	reverse of S&P 500 returns with no dividend reinvestment from 2000 to
2002	67	-0.73%	$1,098,371	$ (65,000)	-23.37%	$440,680	$ (65,000)	2017. Data obtained from the Federal Reserve database in St. Louis (FRED)
2003	68	11.39%	$1,158,475	$ (65,000)	26.38%	$491,932	$ (65,000)	and reported by New York University - Source: https://pages.stern.nyu.edu
2004	69	29.60%	$1,436,384	$ (65,000)	8.99%	$471,156	$ (65,000)	(Does not include deductions for investment fees)
2005	70	13.41%	$1,564,003	$ (65,000)	3.00%	$420,291	$ (65,000)	
2006	71	0.00%	$1,499,003	$ (65,000)	13.62%	$412,535	$ (65,000)	
2007	72	12.78%	$1,625,575	$ (65,000)	3.53%	$362,097	$ (65,000)	2.) Year - end account value after withdraws plus gain/losses.
2008	73	23.45%	$1,941,773	$ (65,000)	-38.49%	$157,726	$ (65,000)	
2009	74	-38.49%	$1,129,384	$ (65,000)	23.45%	$129,713	$ (65,000)	
2010	75	3.53%	$1,104,252	$ (65,000)	12.78%	$81,290	$ (65,000)	
2011	76	13.62%	$1,189,651	$ (65,000)	0.00%	$16,290	$ (65,000)	
2012	77	3.00%	$1,160,340	$ (65,000)	13.41%	($0)	$ (18,475)	
2013	78	8.99%	$1,199,655	$ (65,000)	29.60%	$0	$0	
2014	79	26.38%	$1,451,124	$ (65,000)	11.39%	$0	$0	
2015	80	-23.37%	$1,046,996	$ (65,000)	-0.73%	$0	$0	
2016	81	-13.04%	$845,468	$ (65,000)	9.54%	$0	$0	
2017	82	-10.14%	$694,737	$ (65,000)	19.42%	$0	$0	
				$ (1,170,000.00)			$ (798,475.00)	
				$ 1,864,737				

Source: Http://pages.stern.nyu.edu (Does not include deductions for investment fees)

Figure 18[1]

The Jones' withdraw nearly $1.2 million and have approximately $700,000 left at age 82. The Smiths aren't so lucky. They withdraw $700,000 of income and run out of money at age 76. The only difference is the order of the market gains and losses—and that's a *huge* difference. Mr. & Mrs. Jones are pretty happy, but the Smiths are not happy at all.

Someone should have told the Smiths about sequence of returns risk when they were investing their money. Sequence of returns doesn't matter when you are in the accumulation phase of retirement, but it makes a big difference in the decumulation phase. That's yet another reason why it's a good idea to work with a financial professional—especially one that also helps you with your decumulation strategy. Make sure your financial planner has a solution to this problem. Ask your advisor, "What solution do you have for sequence of returns risk?" If they don't have an answer, find someone who *does* have a solution.

To solve this problem, the Smiths could have used an indexed annuity (acquired through an insurance company) to eliminate losses. Fixed-index annuities can be complex, and insurance carriers offer different product features. An indexed annuity offers a minimum guaranteed interest rate combined with an interest rate linked to a market index such as the S&P 500. There are other types of annuities (e.g., fixed and variable), but in this discussion, we will stick to fixed-index annuities. I want you to understand how a fixed-index annuity can be a great addition to your retirement portfolio (although it shouldn't be the only product you have).

Figure 19 presents a scenario in which Mr. & Mrs. Smith have a solution for negative annual returns. In this scenario, wherever the annual return is negative, we replace it with a zero. That's how fixed-indexed annuities work. When the market is negative, you earn zero percent. When the market is positive, some or all of the interest is credited to your account, depending on the caps and spreads of your annuity. A cap places a cap on the interest your annuity can earn. For example, if the index earns 12 percent and your annuity has a 10 percent cap, you get 10 percent, not 12 percent. A spread is a percentage subtracted from the change in the index before interest is calculated. For example, if the index increases by 5 percent and there is a 2 percent spread, the interest credited is 3 percent. Figure 19 shows that the Smiths withdrew almost $1.2 million and had more than $2 million left at age 82. What a big difference eliminating volatility makes!

		Mr. & Mrs. Jones			Mr. & Mrs. Smith			
Year	Age	Annual Return	Portfolio Year-End Value	Withdrawals	Annual Return [1]	Portfolio Year-End Value [2]	Withdrawals	Explanation
2000	65	19.42%	$1,129,200	$ (65,000)	-10.14%	$833,600	$ (65,000)	1.) S&P 500 returns with no dividend reinvestment from 2017 - 2000 in reverse of S&P 500 returns with no dividend reinvestment from 2000 to 2017. Data obtained from the Federal Reserve database in St. Louis (FRED) and reported by New York University - Source: https://pages.stern.nyu.edu (Does not include deductions for investment fees)
2001	66	9.54%	$1,171,926	$ (65,000)	-13.04%	$659,899	$ (65,000)	
2002	67	-0.73%	$1,098,371	$ (65,000)	-23.37%	$440,680	$ (65,000)	
2003	68	11.39%	$1,158,475	$ (65,000)	26.38%	$491,932	$ (65,000)	
2004	69	29.60%	$1,436,384	$ (65,000)	8.99%	$471,156	$ (65,000)	
2005	70	13.41%	$1,564,003	$ (65,000)	3.00%	$420,291	$ (65,000)	
2006	71	0.00%	$1,499,003	$ (65,000)	13.62%	$412,535	$ (65,000)	
2007	72	12.78%	$1,625,575	$ (65,000)	3.53%	$362,097	$ (65,000)	2.) Year - end account value after withdraws plus gain/losses.
2008	73	23.45%	$1,941,773	$ (65,000)	-38.49%	$157,726	$ (65,000)	
2009	74	-38.49%	$1,129,384	$ (65,000)	23.45%	$129,713	$ (65,000)	
2010	75	3.53%	$1,104,252	$ (65,000)	12.78%	$81,290	$ (65,000)	
2011	76	13.62%	$1,189,651	$ (65,000)	0.00%	$16,290	$ (65,000)	
2012	77	3.00%	$1,160,340	$ (65,000)	13.41%	($0)	$ (18,475)	
2013	78	8.99%	$1,199,655	$ (65,000)	29.60%	$0	$0	
2014	79	26.38%	$1,451,124	$ (65,000)	11.39%	$0	$0	
2015	80	-23.37%	$1,046,996	$ (65,000)	-0.73%	$0	$0	
2016	81	-13.04%	$845,468	$ (65,000)	9.54%	$0	$0	
2017	82	-10.14%	$694,737	$ (65,000)	19.42%	$0	$0	
				$ (1,170,000.00)			$ (798,475.00)	
				$ 1,864,737				

Source: Http://pages.stern.nyu.edu (Does not include deductions for investment fees)

Figure 19[2]

How much money should you put into a fixed-index annuity? That depends on your individual situation. How much of your portfolio do you want protected from market volatility? How much income do you need to cover your expenses? Most people choose to put a third to half of their portfolio into this type of annuity, depending on their risk tolerance. Add up your Social Security and pension. Subtract the total from your expenses. The result is the amount of income you need to replace. For some people, income might not be a concern—they just want protection for when the market is down.

For those who are concerned about income, you can buy an income rider for a fee. An income rider continues to pay you even if your account balance goes to zero. You can also annuitize the contract, which makes the annuity behave the same way as a pension. You give up the asset, but you receive income until the day you die or for a certain time period. There are a few different options when annuitizing. A fixed-income annuity is good for everyone—both those looking for income and those only looking for market downside protection.

Annuities, life insurance, and investments all have a place in your retirement portfolio. The trick is to create balance in the portfolio and have different levers you can pull. For example, if the stock market is down, you can use money from your life insurance policy and your annuity and keep your investments in the market; this strategy allows you to minimize your sequence of returns risk. It's important to work with an advisor who can help you accumulate *and* decumulate your assets.

I hope that you enjoyed reading this book and that you have started planning a new relationship with money. I wish you much success in everything that you do.

If you would like further guidance to help you with the strategies in this book, reach out to me at my website: **www.dsfinancialstrategies.com** or
call me at 215-660-0288
to schedule an appointment.

END NOTES

Chapter 2

1. Florence Scovel Shinn, *The Game of Life and How to Play It* (reprinted by Sound Wisdom, 2019). Original copyright by Florence Scovel Shinn, 1925.

Chapter 3

1. "How much does a financial advisor make in Philadelphia, PA?" *Glassdoor* (website), accessed April 13, 2023, https://www.glassdoor.com/Salaries/philadelphia-financial-advisor-salary-SRCH_IL.0,12_IM676_KO13,30.htm.

Chapter 5

1. The five biggest money blocks (Snappy Kraken).

Chapter 6

1. Kinniry Jr., F., Jaconetti, C., DiJoseph, M., Walker, D., and Quinn, M. "Putting a value on your value: Quantifying Vanguard Advisor's Alpha˚," *Advisor's Alpha˚ Perspectives*, (July 2022): 1. https://advisors.vanguard.com/iwe/pdf/IARCQAA.pdf.

Chapter 7
1.   The five different money personality types (Snappy Kraken).

Chapter 8
1.   "Ed Slott's elite IRA advisor group," *America's IRA Experts* (website), accessed April 13, 2023, https://www.irahelp.com/about-ed-slotts-elite-ira-advisor-group.

Chapter 9
1.   1. Money myths (Snappy Kraken)
2.   Robert H. Shmerling, "Right brain/left brain, right?" *Mind and Mood* (blog), *Harvard Health Publishing*, March 24, 2022, https://www.health.harvard.edu/blog/right-brainleft-brain-right-2017082512222.

Chapter 11
1.   [Figure 2] (Undebt.it).
2.   [Figure 3] (Undebt.it).

Chapter 12
1.   [Figure 4] Invest with Evidence (Powerpoint by Efficient Advisors, 2020).
2.   [Figure 5] Invest with Evidence (Powerpoint by Efficient Advisors, 2020).
3.   [Figure 6] Invest with Evidence (Powerpoint by Efficient Advisors, 2020).
4.   "Helmet Statistics," *Bicycle Helmet Safety Institute* (website), accessed April 13, 2023, https://helmets.org/stats.htm.
5.   Time Magazine, 3/9/2009
6.   Warren Buffett quote

7.   [Figure 6] Invest with Evidence (Powerpoint by Efficient Advisors, 2020).

8.   William F. Sharpe, "Likely gains from market timing," *Financial Analysts Journal*, (1975)31:2, 60–69, https://doi.org/10.2469/faj.v31.n2.60.

9.   [Figure 7] Invest with Evidence (Powerpoint by Efficient Advisors, 2020).

10. Damon Darlin, "It's time to ignore advice about which stocks to buy in 2017," *The New York Times*, January 4, 2017, https://www.nytimes.com/2017/01/04/upshot/its-time-to-ignore-advice-about-which-stocks-to-buy-in-2017.html.

11. Hendrik Bessembinder, "Do stocks outperform treasury bills?" *Journal of Financial Economics*, (2018:9)129:3, 440–457, https://doi.org/10.1016/j.jfineco.2018.06.004.

12. "The Jack Bogle legacy: The American College remembers former trustee and industry icon," *The American College of Financial Services* (website), January 23, 2019, https://www.theamericancollege.edu/news-center/the-jack-bogle-legacy-the-american-college-remembers-former-trustee-and-industry-icon.

13. Smart Money Magazine, 2006.

14. [Figure 8] Invest with Evidence (Powerpoint by Efficient Advisors, 2020).

15. "Confessions of a former mutual funds reporter," Fortune Magazine, April 26, 1999.

16. [Figure 9] Invest with Evidence (Powerpoint by Efficient Advisors, 2020).

17. [Figure 10] Invest with Evidence (Powerpoint by Efficient Advisors, 2020).

18. [Figure 11] Fortune Magazine, 1999.

19.   [Figure 12] Invest with Evidence (Powerpoint by Efficient Advisors, 2020).

20.   [Figure 13] Invest with Evidence (Powerpoint by Efficient Advisors, 2020).

21.   [Figure 14] Invest with Evidence (Powerpoint by Efficient Advisors, 2020).

22.   Alex Rosenberg, "The inspiring story of the worst market timer ever," Trading Nation (blog), CNBC, August 27, 2015, https://www.cnbc.com/2015/08/27/the-inspiring-story-of-the-worst-market-timer-ever.html.

23.   Capital Group/American Funds 2019 study

24.   Chad Creveling, "Vanguard study shows how advisors can add 3% or more to your annual investment return," ChadCreveling's Blog (blog), Seeking Alpha, June 19, 2014, https://seekingalpha.com/instablog/1347881-chadcreveling/3005453-vanguard-study-shows-how-advisors-can-add-3-percent-or-more-to-your-annual-investment-return.

Chapter 14

1.   "Life insurance retirement supplement: Manage your retirement income with life insurance," Ohio National Financial Services, 2020.

2.   "Life insurance retirement supplement: Manage your retirement income with life insurance," Ohio National Financial Services (2020): 3.

3.   "Life insurance retirement supplement: Manage your retirement income with life insurance," Ohio National Financial Services (2020): 4.

4.   "Life insurance retirement supplement: Manage your retirement income with life insurance," Ohio National Financial Services (2020): 5.

5.   "Life insurance retirement supplement: Manage your retirement income with life insurance," Ohio National Financial Services (2020): 7.

ACKNOWLEDGEMENTS

First and foremost, I want to thank God. You have guided me through all my days, the light and the dark and made me the woman I am today.

Thank you to my family, friends, and colleagues. I love you guys.

Thank you to Cheli Grace and the Books to Millions® team for helping me bring this book out into the world.

Thank you to Don Blanton, Ed Slott, David McKnight. I have learned some much which has helped me and my clients.

Thank you, Steve Miller, Zack Shepard, Alex Rodriguez, and Sabrina Williams for teaching me the Evidence Based Investing principles.

A special thank you to my Fem City® family.

Thank you to my spiritual teacher, Lynn Rene Macdonald. The prayer you taught me changed my life and countless others.

ABOUT THE AUTHOR

Photo courtesy of Marikate Venuto.

D awn Santoriello is a CFP® professional and the founder and
CEO of DS Financial Strategies, a fee-based financial planning
firm that develops customized plans
designed to maximize the efficiency of
your money.

Born in Brooklyn, New York, and
raised in Long Island, Dawn graduated
from Adelphi University with a BS in
Finance. She currently lives in Yardley, Pennsylvania. Away from
the office, you can find Dawn living true to her wellness and wealth
lifestyle by hiking, kayaking, mountain biking, and meditating.

Dawn is the former host of *Conquer Your Finances, Conquer
Your Life* on RVN TV. She has been published in numerous blogs
and journals, including *Wealth Planning Advisor* and *Let's Talk Philadelphia*. She has also been featured in *Forbes, Investment Advisor,
Market Watch*, and *The Philadelphia Inquirer*. She is a member of
Ed Slott's Elite Advisor Group. This exclusive group is comprised
of nearly 400 of the nation's top financial professionals who are
dedicated to ongoing training and mastery of advanced retirement

account and tax planning laws and strategies. She is also a member of David McKnight's Power of Zero Advisory Group.

Be sure to check out Dawn's YouTube page (DS Financial Strategies) for "Financial Fridays with Dawn." For more information or to get in touch with Dawn, please visit:

www.dsfinancialstrategies.com

HELP ME INSPIRE AND EDUCATE OTHERS!

Thank you for reading my book! As you know I am on a mission to help others achieve their financial goals with peace of mind.

There are several ways that you can play a role in this mission:

1. Leave a review on Amazon.
Book reviews help books show up in search results and help others decide if they want to read the book. Please take two minutes to leave a helpful review on Amazon.

2. Give a copy to a friend.
If you like this book and you have friends or colleagues who might benefit from it, it's a gift that can change lives. This book helps spread the word about building wealth and manifesting your dreams.

3. Invite me to speak.
I love to share my stories and help others become efficient with their money. For speaking requests go to my website at: www.dsfinancialstrategies.com and send a request or call me at 215-660-0288

4. Join my newsletter.

Sign-up for my newsletter to get updates to events and information. You can you to my website and sign up on the home page at: www. dsfinancialstrategies.com

5. Meet me at our exclusive Manifest and Invest Retreats.

We currently have our Manifest and Invest Retreats in the beautiful Caribbean Island of the Bahamas. Get on the waitlist and join us for a life-changing experience filled with fun and adventure.

Email me at: Dawn@manifestninvest.com

www.ingramcontent.com/pod-product-compliance
Lightning Source LLC
Chambersburg PA
CBHW070712130626
46553CB00005B/1960